The Most Scenic Roads in Massachusetts

THE
MOST
Scenic
ROADS in
MASSACHUSETTS

20 Routes Off the Beaten Path

John Gibson

DOWN EAST BOOKS

Camden · Maine

Front cover photograph: In the Berkshires,
on Route 41 in Mt. Washington State Forest.

Cover photograph © 1997 by Kindra Clineff

Library of Congress Control Number: 2002109184

Design by Phil Schirmer

Printed and bound at Versa Press, Inc., E. Peoria, Ill.

2 4 5 3 1

 DOWN EAST BOOKS / CAMDEN, MAINE
www.downeastbooks.com

Remembering
BARBARA ANN MATTINA,
artist, singer of songs,
dear friend

contents

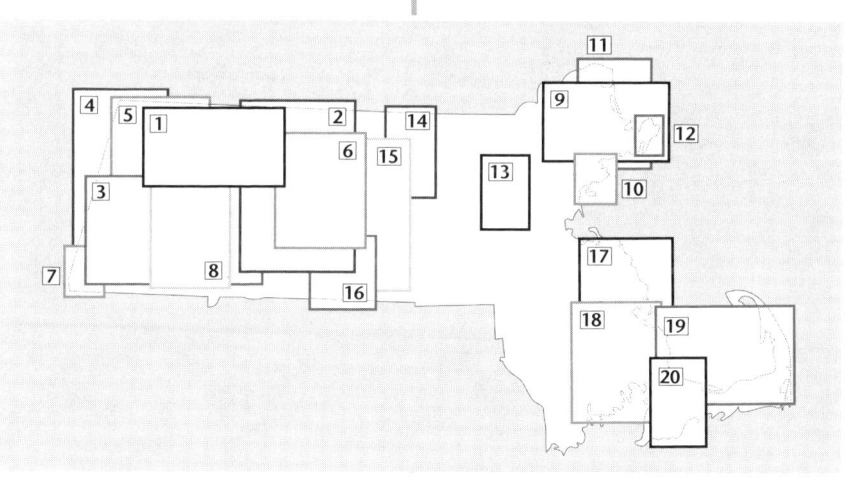

The Most Scenic Roads in Massachusetts

An Introduction

What does one say about Massachusetts, one of the smallest states of these fifty United? A state involved in so many important moments of American history, so intimately bound up with the great democratic experiment? How explain a small, northeastern place with limited natural resources, but so blessed for centuries with an astonishing, buoyant human capital that its contributions to government, science, commerce, education, technology, the arts, and world affairs brook few comparisons? And how convey the uniqueness of such a place, its geographic reality more interesting and diverse than even the most generous of encomiums over the years have made known? To sing this Commonwealth's praises one must first accept that it is and shall ever be a place of magnificent paradox, urban yet mainly rural, coastal but often mountainous, industrial but wooded and unspoiled, dense yet scattered and separate, sophisticated but without pretense.

The state takes its name from that small tribe of Indians who established themselves in the shadows of Great Blue Hill, one of several tribes to whom white arrivals would owe their very survival and then later seek to extirpate. An organized, complex, and efficient Indian society characterized many parts of the Bay State when people of England and Europe first descended on its shores. These same aboriginal peoples of Massachusetts had likely earlier seen the ships of Norsemen coasting their shoreline before those Norse sailors returned north to far Atlantic Canada. There is a little stone on the banks of the Charles River in Cambridge, which suggests, perhaps apocryphally, that Leif Eriksson stepped ashore there in 1011.

The Most Scenic Roads in Massachusetts

In the 1600s the real torrent began. Europeans came to Massachusetts in increasing numbers, and every American schoolchild since has been fed the doubtful stuff of Plymouth Rock. Once established, white settlers fell to the making of community in earnest, and Massachusetts would establish a manner for the country. The Bay State is, after all, the birthplace of dozens of essential statesmen and four American Presidents including the Adamses, father and son, citizens of south-shore Quincy, immensely influential in shaping the early republic.

English Puritans brought schooling to Massachusetts with a first, primitive academy in 1635, their efforts surviving today in the form of prestigious Boston Latin. Free public education, albeit of a demanding and intolerant sort, had been established here by 1647. Bay Staters planted the seeds of some of the finest institutions of higher education early and well. In 1638, along the Charles, the Reverend John Harvard fostered the growth of a tiny college for religious training, which has grown some since. Massachusetts has latterly become home to dozens of colleges and universities, many of them ranked as the most prestigious in the country, perhaps even the world.

From early days, this has been a place where the creative flourish, and one where those with a certain view of public life have scattered their influence. Massachusetts, heir to the Bay Colony, has reliably generated singular, important minds the way some states generate wheat. From such early civic forces as John Winthrop, William Bradford, or Josiah Quincy, to fiery Puritan divines in the mold of Cotton Mather, to latter-day *philosophes* such as Emerson, Thoreau, and Transcendentalists Bronson Alcott and Margaret Fuller, to scientists and educators like William James and the Lowells and Eliots of Harvard, or to poets Emily Dickinson and e e cummings, the Bay State's famous sons and daughters have stocked the biography shelves at the Boston Public Library to overflowing. And they keep coming. The result has been a state where ideas flourish, collide, and compete, their product somehow essential to the country.

The Most Scenic Roads in Massachusetts

The civic energies of this place flourished early. By their fireside in England, John Winthrop and his wife decided one winter night in 1629 to risk their fortunes in the New World; England in the reign of Archbishop Laud had become an unwelcoming place for Puritans. Winthrop would ascend to Governorship of the Massachusetts Bay Colony and leave his imprint forever on Boston. More of his stripe would desert England and follow. Winthrop's Puritan sentiments would be echoed in the sermons of many a Puritan divine, perhaps most notably in the words of the Reverend Cotton Mather, scientist, member of the Royal Society, and minister to souls. Hot on Mather's heels would come young Jonathan Edwards, leading the Great Awakening of spirituality that so fervently swept western Massachusetts in the 1730s. Others, like William Ellery Channing, whose voice awakened souls on Sunday mornings at Boston's Arlington Street Church, would feed the Bay State's growing penchant for humanitarian causes and the abolition of slavery. A long row of statuary on Boston Common's Tremont Street promenade reads like a Who's Who of early American social conscience. The tradition of thoughtful dissent is long here, perhaps a legacy of Puritan seriousness and right thinking leavened by educated tolerance.

Massachusetts afforded the luxury of education and experimentation with higher forms of social order by being, early and late, a place where practical ideas could be turned into manufactured wealth. (Philosopher Thoreau, after all, benefited from his father's detested pencil manufactory; and even Hawthorne toiled at Salem harbor to provide necessary income.) The great textile mills of Lowell and Lawrence dominated the commercial arena, their looms churning forth product for decades in a way that echoed but leapt beyond similar epochs in the English midlands. Boston Harbor and its connection to the wider world supported a burgeoning merchant class. The Bay State's economy roared forward in what historians Richard Brown and Jack Trager have called "a record of thousands of small successes, dozens of which were truly spectacular."

The Most Scenic Roads in Massachusetts

The state's great rivers provided motive power, and local genius devised ways to exploit it. The river valleys of the state sprouted factories of all sorts—some adapted today to new enterprise or utterly transformed into R&D centers, offices, studios, or massive fine art venues, some a part of Massachusetts' ever-growing service economy. In the modern era, too, the Bay State has been home to a band of brilliant tinkerers at General Electric's Lynn plant who produced America's first reliable jet engine, and not far away, in Cambridge, a fellow by the name of Land set up a lab to produce something called the Polaroid Land camera. Always, the state has paid its way with a certain brilliance.

Massachusetts's frontage on the Atlantic, nearly fifteen hundred miles in length if one could pull this coast into a straight line, has inevitably played a large role in its fortunes. The Atlantic was the highway by which the English, French, Portuguese, and others made commercial haste to New England and on which the West Indies trade flourished, with Boston as its northern gateway. For centuries, this coast supported a robust fishing industry. It still does in places such as Gloucester and New Bedford, though fishing has lately become a precarious enterprise, its coffers ratcheting from near shutdown to temporary plenty as the government-limited catch is adjusted in an effort to preserve threatened stocks. While fishing grew as a way of life for many, so did the legendary boatbuilding shops that served both fishermen and sea merchants. Some of these still exist, as a drive past Lowell's boatshop on the banks of the Merrimack in Amesbury will testify. In the modern era of steel vessels, Quincy's massive yards turned out ship after ship for the war effort against the Axis powers.

Railroads nurtured the Bay State's prosperity as well, enterprising little lines reaching every corner of New England, but always connecting with Boston, the hub of a Yankee universe. In his cabin at Walden Pond, Thoreau could hear the passing trains of the fledgling Boston and Concord Railroad a ways off through the woods. There was a time when a traveler could board a sleeping car of an evening in Boston and awake to breakfast in the Canadian Maritimes, Montreal, or Washington. Remnants of the tracks of these several railroads are still found in unexpected corners of the state, reminders of the marvelous services that have since been lost to us.

Massachusetts has long been a place of distinct communities and neighborhoods, each with a flavor and ambience all its own. Starting with Dame Boston, a city of highly defined enclaves and a politics to go with them, out to a varied ring of suburban towns, and then on to rural, central and western Massachusetts, one notices as one travels the unique flavor of places that might all be the same but are not. And the changes are sometimes abrupt, from city to country, flatland to hill towns, river valleys to mountain range, ethnic neighborhood to polyglot city in a matter of a few miles. Differences between localities are not merely geographic or topographic in the Bay State; they are often reflective of economics and nationality. Eastern Massachusetts, particularly, has seen wave upon wave of immigration roll through its towns and cities. First the English, then northern European, then the Irish, then Italians and Portuguese, then Asians, then Middle Easterners, then those from the Caribbean. Each group brought its own politics of improvement. Names like Honey Fitz, James Michael Curley, Dapper O'Neil, Endicott Peabody, Leverett Saltonstall, and hundreds of others are forever etched on the body politic.

For a small state, Massachusetts has had more experience with the heady mix of national culture, diverse political fortune, and varying public sentiment than many states twice its size. It has made this unique experience a virtue. And if the flavor of a certain political view has occasionally dominated local identity, religion, too, has sometimes defined parts of Massachusetts. The early politics of first settlements were primarily religious here, after all. For those who have grown up here, there is a clear recollection of various towns being known as Catholic or Protestant, or of distinct neighborhoods being Jewish or Portuguese or Oriental, or of places like Southie or Back Bay or Beacon Hill. Whatever the obvious limitations of such labels, they reflect the Bay Stater's sense of how people have organized themselves around nationality, religion, sometimes race, economic status, politics, and other deeply binding concerns.

Geographically, Massachusetts defies all complacent expectations. It is seashore and marsh, river valley and upland, wooded plain and mountain range, mainland and—in the form of Nantucket and Martha's Vineyard—island civilization. Since we are out for a drive, it is this unique geography, quite drenched in history, that matters. Navigating Massachusetts roads, the traveler soon finds that this state is a place of rivers— the Connecticut, the Deerfield, the Merrimack, the Westfield, the Housatonic, and more—and that highways follow, cross, and rejoin them as the whims of terrain dictate.

Beyond the distinctive, flat coastal zone, a salty region still visibly marked by the retreat of glacial ice, Massachusetts rises westward in alternating rows of low hills and riverine lowlands. For travelers, interest mounts as one background is exchanged for another, river for hill country, with small towns and modest cities peppering the landscape in between. The larger rivers once gave Massachusetts not only energy to run its great mills, but a north-south commerce as well. The Connecticut River, one remembers, linked the western precincts of the state with Vermont, New Hampshire, and Connecticut as an artery of river-borne exchange. The Merrimack has come down from New Hampshire and served similarly. In the center of the state are great reservoirs. Thirty-nine-square-mile, manmade Quabbin is the largest and certainly the greatest of Massachusetts's nearly fourteen hundred inland water bodies. The flooded ghosts of whole communities repose on the bottom, under Quabbin's cold waters.

Beyond its center, Massachusetts climbs steadily to the west, the endless fortress wall of the Berkshires crossing the state from north to south as the Bay State's contribution to the magnificent Appalachian chain. This country beyond the Connecticut River, topped by brooding, 3,491-foot

Mount Greylock, reminds the traveler of its lofty neighbor states to the north, and in these hills are places as wild and unspoiled as any in the northeast. Writer Herman Melville lived in the shadow of Greylock and dreamed of whales. Here the Appalachian Scenic Trail, the longest hiking path in eastern America, crosses hill after hill, pausing in the occasional sheltered valley town before marching farther up the map.

In defiance of common perception, Massachusetts is often a place of rural occupations. Driving through the Connecticut River Valley, one sees great flatlands dotted with tobacco barns and cornfields. Sandwiched between high-tech research and manufacturing centers along Route 2 are broad fields full of produce in season. In central Massachusetts, Route 2 vistas include rolling farms with cattle in fields and sleek horses cantering in paddocks. The high rib of west-central Massachusetts is by any measure orchard country, with beckoning roadside stands selling autumn's sweet apple cider and frequent injunctions to "pick your own." And, as one rolls west through the high ground of the Berkshires, one finds many small maple syrup producers lodged in hill farms near woodlots logged for lumber. Wherever the journey, with so varied a landscape, Massachusetts absorbs and consistently engages the traveler in ways as often rural as urban. Travel is a pleasure here.

PRACTICALITIES

The Most Scenic Roads of Massachusetts provides a detailed introduction to twenty routes of travel, from shorter trips to long excursions, that take the driver through the state's most appealing natural terrain and along corridors of history in one of America's most interesting places. Though any route in these pages can be covered in a matter of a few hours, such is the attractiveness of the Massachusetts countryside that hours become pleasant, engaging days as the inviting communities, institutions, museums, parks, woodlands, and galleries ever draw one in.

The Most Scenic Roads in Massachusetts

With a nod to the unique history and distinctive geography of the state, *The Most Scenic Roads of Massachusetts* explores many a rural Massachusetts back road, follows hidden rivers, and circles ponds, lakes, and uplands at will. Our definition of "scenic" is necessarily elastic in a state so varied as to settlement, terrain, and history. Sometimes scenic means wild, isolated, and mountainous, as when driving to the tiny, high-country hamlet of Mount Washington on the New York border. Or scenic may mean settled, busy, and perched on a fine expanse of Atlantic shore in neighborhoods thick with the artifacts of New England history, as when we ride out to Marblehead.

Many drives in this book begin in or near major towns or cities and quickly jump into quiet countryside, exploring stretches of highway seen by few. Others thread through more populous ground, connecting with important points of regional history, architecture, ocean-going shoreland, and bright little seaside communities. Still others get lost in woods and cranberry bog country while roaming the Bay State's hidden south shore or explore quiet towns along the New Hampshire border. Each route in this volume has been framed to please both the eye and the mind, and to reintroduce into driving an idea that is almost totally missing in the mad hurry of many lives; that is, actually *seeing* the countryside through which we pass and *appreciating* what it tells us about both past and present in the very center of New England.

In other books in this series (*Maine's Most Scenic Roads* and *New Hampshire's Most Scenic Roads*), I have urged users of these guides to make a few practical adjustments in the name of comfortable travel. They deserve repeating here. First, despite having its share of highly developed urban centers, a great deal of the Bay State is rural, quiet, and prone to going to bed early. There are many towns on routes described in these pages where you will be disappointed if you expect to find food, fuel, and other amenities in late evenings. Places like the Berkshires or the Cape are heavily booked in the summer months, and accommodations should be chosen and reserved early, where possible. Finding a comfortable base at an inn central to a given region can be a good solution when exploring countryside in various directions. Even when camping, reservations for space ought to be booked well ahead.

It's a sensible idea to have your car maintained before setting out on these leisurely Bay State road trips, with special attention to tire pressure and engine timing. Both make a difference in fuel miles-per-gallon. If you have a choice, travel in a smaller, fuel-efficient car rather than the gas-gulping SUV on the far side of the driveway. Touring is more enjoyable without a guilty conscience, and with fuel-efficient travel we'll all breathe a little easier.

The maps in this book are more than adequate for following the routes described here, but a road atlas also may be useful to put these route maps into a larger context. For your safety, take time to review the route map of each drive before you set out rather than when you're rounding a tight curve. A *calibrated* dashboard compass provides an in-fallible assist when someone in the back seat asserts that you are lost and that north is south.

Enjoy the journey.

LORE AND LEGEND

Whether you hail from the Bay State or are an intentional traveler here, a certain pleasure is gained from learning more about Massachusetts before taking to the back roads. Americans too often tend to travel blind, to know little of their chosen destinations, especially when abroad, and to miss much of the flavor of places visited. There is a simple antidote. A trip to the local used bookstore or public library will pay dividends to the traveler who likes to savor the journey twice, once while reading about it and again later, while cruising the backcountry.

Massachusetts fairly drips with history, and having a sense of that history serves to put exploration in context. *Massachusetts: A Concise History* is a highly readable, shorter history of the Bay State by Richard Brown and Jack Trager, professors of history at the universities of Connecticut and Massachusetts respectively. This fine volume bears the stamp of the professional historian but reads comfortably, without the usual heavy going. Howard Russell's *Indian New England Before the Mayflower* provides a fascinating glimpse of the highly developed native cultures present here before white men lumbered ashore. The doyen of American maritime historians, Samuel Elliot Morrison, has provided a look at seagoing matters in his *The Maritime History of Massachusetts: 1783–1860,* and his *Builders of the Bay Colony* covers significant figures in the early days of Massachusetts settlement. Darrett Rutman's *Winthrop's Boston* provides a picture of the great capital in its formative days during the time of one of its most important leaders. Harvard historian Oscar Handlin's seminal *Boston's Immigrants* provides a view of the contributions to the Bay State of the many from afar who came here. *King Philip's War,* by Eric Schultz and Michael Tougias, offers a view of the earliest settlers' conflicts with natives and recounts the tragic killing of Chief Massasoit's son and the war with the Wampanoag, a major event in the history of southeastern and central Massachusetts.

One of the drives in this book roams by the replica of Henry David Thoreau's cabin at Walden Pond, and reading *Walden* and *Civil Disobedience* makes a good preparation for a reflective walk around the Walden Pond reservation. In the same drive you will pass scenes mentioned in Thoreau's *A Week on the Concord and Merrimack Rivers*, a personal, informal story. Roderick Peattie's *The Berkshires: The Purple Hills* collects essays by Haydn Mason, Walter Prichard Eaton, and others in a fine, detailed introduction to the state's westernmost precincts. It's the kind of pleasant regional writing that would never get published today. *Massachusetts: The WPA Guide to Massachusetts*, originally released in 1937 and since reprinted by Northeastern University Press, is still a useful, comprehensive guide to the character of the state. Old Harvardian David McCord's *About Boston: Sight, Sound, Flavor and Inflection,* if you can find a copy, is a charming recounting of the place by the late poet and essayist.

Henry Beston's *Outermost House* has long been a classic introduction to the serene mysteries of the outer Cape; Henry David Thoreau's *Cape Cod* captured a vanished sense of that place, and Henry Crocker Kittredge's flavorful *Cape Cod: Its People and Their History* reappeared with a new introduction in 1995. In the same league is Joseph Lincoln's crusty *Cape Cod Yesterdays,* and for Cape Ann and the North Shore, one cannot help but value *Cape Ann: Cape America* by former *Boston Globe* editor and columnist Herbert Kenny. Though not solely about Massachusetts places, George Francis Marlowe's pleasantly eccentric (and hard to find) *Byroads of Old New England* is an interesting pointer to rural places of note.

Those interested in natural history and geology will find Barbara Blau Chamberlain's *These Fragile Outposts,* a fine guide to Cape Cod and the Islands. Greg O'Brien covers some of the same ground in his newer book, *A Guide to Nature on Cape Cod and the Islands.* Beth Schwartzman's excellent *The Nature of Cape Cod* is also a superb guide to the Cape's natural features. The natural world of the Berkshires is covered in the pages of *The Berkshires,* noted earlier. Neil Jorgenson's *Sierra Club Naturalist's Guide to Southern New England* is a useful modern perennial. The *National Audubon Society Field Guide to New England* helps with plant, tree, and flower identification while you're doing your roadside exploring. Those interested in discovering who lived where amongst Bay State *littérateurs* while driving country roads will enjoy William Corbett's enjoyable survey *Literary New England.*

For those who will get out of the car and take to the hills, John Brady and Brian White have provided all the information you'll need in *50 Hikes in Massachusetts,* a handy hiker's guide that covers the entire state. Robert Finch's *Outlands* offers an outdoor writer's discerning view of the Cape by a long-time habitué. Those who begin the Hingham-to-Plymouth drive in eastern Massachusetts with a visit to World's End Reservation will find Sheila Connor's *New England Natives* interesting, especially in its references to the work of Frederick Law Olmsted. Massachusetts's five national wildlife refuges are described in the *Audubon Guide to the National Wildlife Refuges: New England.*

1

Route
Greenfield to North Adams

Highway
MA 10, US 5, Shelburne Falls Road, MA 2

Distance
50.5 miles

The northwestern corner of Massachusetts is home to fine hill country, a place of rolling uplands, working farms, and dense, stony hills carpeted in leafy hardwoods. Here are the Bay State's highest elevations, some offering sweeping perspectives over the western third of Massachusetts and into Vermont, Connecticut, or eastern New York. The traveler here experiences a region of Massachusetts that has more in common with other rural New England neighborhoods than with the precincts of great cities like Boston.

This drive begins in the busy city of Greenfield, itself a place worthy of considerable exploration. A fine woodland park that nestles above a broad bend in the Connecticut River dominates its east side. The park is topped by the famous Poets Seat. Downtown, the city's center is vibrant, and there are historic sites that date back to the time of early English settlement. Originally an agricultural and shipping village, later a rail hub, and then a manufacturing center, Greenfield has now blossomed as

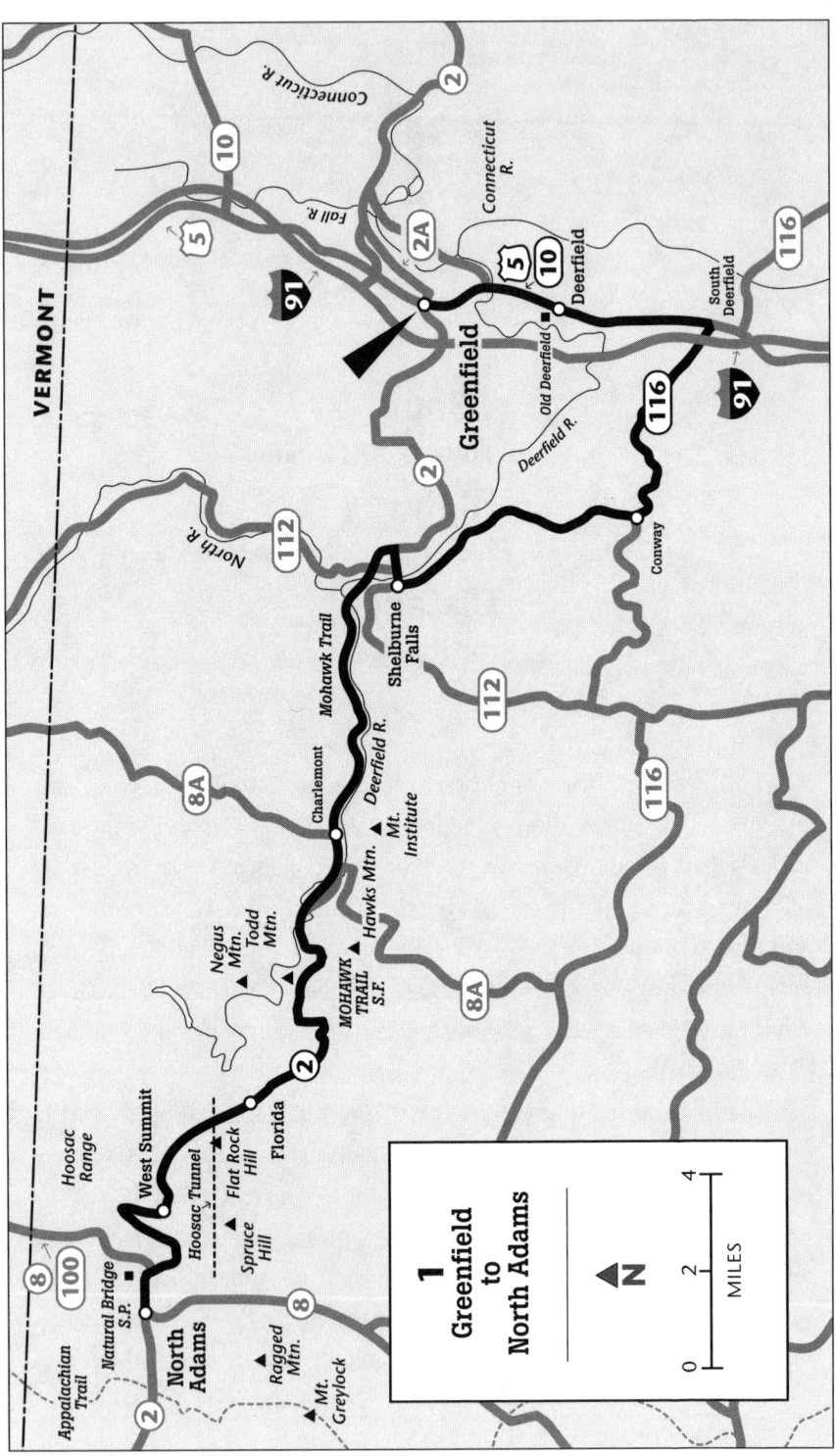

VERMONT

Connecticut R.

Fall R.

North R.

Deerfield R.

Connecticut R.

Appalachian Trail

Hoosac Range

Natural Bridge S.P.

North Adams

Ragged Mtn.

Mt. Greylock

Hoosac Tunnel

West Summit

Flat Rock Hill

Florida

Spruce Hill

Negus Mtn.

Todd Mtn.

MOHAWK TRAIL S.F.

Hawks Mtn.

Mt. Institute

Mohawk Trail

Charlemont

Shelburne Falls

Conway

Greenfield

Old Deerfield

Deerfield

South Deerfield

1
Greenfield
to
North Adams

N

MILES
0   2   4

Route markers: 8, 100, 2, 8, 8A, 112, 116, 8A, 2, 112, 116, 116, 116, 5, 10, 91, 5, 2A, 5, 10, 91

a services center but keeps the lingering, pleasant flavor of a traditional community.

This drive begins at the junction of MA 2A with US 5 and MA 10 in Greenfield's downtown. *Go south* on Routes 5 and 10 toward Deerfield, passing through an older residential neighborhood that hosts the occasional old mill building. You'll cross the Deerfield River next and then go over the Deerfield town line into less settled countryside. Open fields appear to the right backed by woodlands at 2 miles. To the left but partially hidden are the highlands of the Pocumtuck Range.

Watch now on your right for a side road where you *bear right* and then immediately *left* into historic Old Deerfield. This preserved village from colonial times offers a splendid chance to sample an America now long vanished. Here also is the campus of prestigious Deerfield Academy, whose attractive grounds mingle with the broad lawns and massive shade trees of the old community. Little about the tranquil village of today testifies to the near total destruction of this community on two occasions. As a distant outpost remote from Boston, Deerfield suffered greatly during the early years of the settlement. It was wiped out in the Indian raids attendant on King Philip's War in 1675, then again reduced to ashes in the notorious Deerfield Massacre of 1704.

Drive down Old Deerfield Street, park wherever your fancy takes you, and walk around the settlement. Pass the white spire of the First Church of Deerfield, originally founded in 1688. Stroll around the campus of the academy, enjoying the fine colonial and Federal architecture, and give yourself plenty of time here to get a sense of this unique place. There are fifty restored structures in historic Old Deerfield, spread over more than ninety acres. Fourteen restored buildings are open to the public. Tours and special events provide direct access to the way of life once lived here and offer much to entrance fanciers of early Americana. Call ahead or check the web site for information on current programs: (413) 774-5581; www.historic-deerfield.org.

Early morning, Old Deerfield

Old Deerfield Street bends leftward at its foot, and you follow it back out to US 5 and MA 10, *turning right and south* toward South Deerfield. Rolling southward, you are soon in farms and fields passing a series of attractive older houses at just under 5 miles. Trees hug the road, their silhouettes interspersed with cultivated fields, while a line of hills rises to the east. At 7.8 miles, *go sharply right* on MA 116 and head northwest in more open farm country, where you shortly run under I-91.

The road continues northwest at 8.3 miles as a range of hills appears ahead, and you pass through fields of silage corn, cattle, and distinctive old silos. The road winds, passes through dense foliage, and negotiates a series of broad bends as it follows the rocky South River, which lies hidden in a well-worn ravine. You'll cross the Conway town line at 10.7

miles and cross over a series of ribs going northwest. The road opens out and you pass the Conway Grammar School at 12.3 miles, arriving in pretty, diminutive Conway Village by the Inn and Historical Society building at 13.5 miles.

Leave 116 and *go sharply right* here onto Shelburne Falls Road, trending northeast along the meandering South River. This road is blessedly free of traffic, the only likely competition for right-of-way being the occasional milk truck gathering its cargo from local dairy farms. Scattered houses lie back from the road, hidden in the trees, and hobblebush viburnum grows everywhere as you round Catlin Lot Hill on your left and roll northward in the shadow of ridgeland to your right. Stay left at a fork, cross the Bear River soon, and—heading northwest again—leap Schneck Brook at the foot of 1,400-foot Flag Mountain.

You begin a descent in a border of tall trees at 17.8 miles and enter a more settled zone with limited views of the hills ahead. Crossing some railroad tracks, you travel by Gardner's Falls Station Recreation Area at 21 miles and then through a neighborhood of old mills. The Deerfield River is in sight again immediately, near the site of ancient glacial potholes. You next cross a handsome iron latticework bridge at 22.2 miles, emerging on the main street of Shelburne Falls, a pleasant thoroughfare of attractive traditional storefronts and older homes. To the left as you cross the river is the old trolley bridge, now used for pedestrian travel and bright with flowers in summer. Many little New England towns had real main streets like this once upon a time. Take time to savor this one. *Follow 2A east* here and in minutes connect with MA 2, where you *go left and west* on the fabled Mohawk Trail.

On MA 2 you cross the North River and go by the access road to the Shelburne Trolley Museum, heading through woodlands and rolling farm country. Rising through a series of ledgy outcrops at 24.8 miles, you reach a point where there are fine views along the Deerfield River in East Charlemont. Walnut Hill and Snow Mountain yield to 1,500-foot Mount

Institute on your left as you stay with the river. Pass through a neighborhood of old houses, several architecturally distinctive churches, and more good river outlooks at Charlemont, where MA 8A departs northward. Immediately beyond, you pass the entrance to Berkshire East Ski Area at Peak Mountain. Along here, commercial outfitters provide opportunities for whitewater rafting.

Maple sugar operations appear in this stretch of road as maple-laced mountains close in on each side. The Deerfield River drops in its channel to the left of the highway, eventually tumbling northward as the road pulls to the south next to lovely Mohawk Trail State Forest, between Coon Hill and 1,800-foot Hawks Mountain. Formerly a gravel cart road, the Mohawk Trail was first paved in 1914, and one can imagine the demands of the task as this road navigates such angled terrain. You'll cross the Savoy town line at 37 miles with mountain views appearing through the hardwoods as you ascend a series of steep bends and then descend to the banks of the Cold River. You will need to really focus on *driving* here. The route then follows an intervale into the hamlet of Drury and quickly resumes climbing toward Whitcomb Summit in the mysteriously named town of Florida. Hyperbole seems appropriate in these parts. The countryside—mountainous, densely wooded, and cut by boulder-strewn streams—is extraordinarily appealing, a surprise to some who think of Massachusetts as primarily an urban state.

Ascending the nearly 2,200-foot Flat Rock Hill (Brown's Garage motorist services is at 41 miles), you emerge from a series of serpentine curves through gorgelike terrain, passing falling-rock warnings at 43.6 miles. You are over the Hoosac Tunnel now. Buried deep in the mountain, unseen, it is the longest rail tunnel in northeastern America. Slabbing the mountainside, you reach the eastern summit turnout, where you'll have spectacular eastward views from horizon to horizon across ranges of rough, wooded, flat-topped mountains. High up you may be, yet the road climbs still farther, heading west and crossing the road to Savoy Moun-

 The Deerfield River, Shelburne

tain State Forest a few miles to the south, where there is camping in the midst of all this altitude.

You are on the spine of the great Hoosac Range here, and you can sense the altitude, the woods pulling back, and an emerging feeling of openness. But the law of gravity applies, and soon you must climb down, so check your brakes. A turnout at West Summit offers grand views west into New York and northwest over Vermont. The very real descent takes you quickly north down the steep grade of the famous hairpin turn at 46.5 miles, and then back south as the road makes what seems an endless drop into the valley west of the Hoosac Range. You finally sense the valley floor under you at 48.5 miles as you approach North Adams. The Mohawk Trail officially ends at 49.5 miles, and you'll shortly pass MA 8 on your right as it runs north to the Marble Arch stone formation at Natural Bridge State Park. In minutes you come into the center of North Adams, where this drive ends at the Tourist Information Center, 50.3 miles from your departure point in Greenfield.

Spend some time here. In a notch between the hills, North Adams is an interesting old manufacturing and rail hub now reshaping itself as the home of a large art center, a growing state college, an interesting regional museum, and an attractive traditional shopping area. 🦌

Route

Holyoke to Northfield

Highway

US 202, MA 116, MA 47,
Sunderland Road, Turners Falls Road,
Montague Road, Main Road, MA 10, 63

Distance

40.5 miles

Here's a varied drive that takes off from the great conurbation of Holyoke-Chicopee-Springfield-Longmeadow, above the Connecticut state line, and works its way north through west-central Massachusetts to end in the quiet academy town of Northfield on the New Hampshire–Vermont border, just east of what is known as Satan's Kingdom. Along the way the route visits the Holyoke Range, the bustling university and college towns of South Hadley and Amherst, and the rural backcountry that embraces the big, winding Connecticut River up north. The route finds its way through the heart of the upper Pioneer Valley, a place of several ancient rivers, working farms, and an unusually rich cluster of academic institutions and resources.

From anywhere in the Holyoke-Springfield area, proceed through the heavily settled east side of Holyoke, crossing the Connecticut River on US 202, rolling eastward in South Hadley Falls. Begin this route at the junction of US 202 and MA 116 in South Hadley. Set your odometer here, and from 202 *turn north* on MA 116.

North of US 202, 116 winds through the town of South Hadley, very soon passing the remains of an old mill at Stoney Brook and going through the 800-acre grounds of Mount Holyoke College on College Street. Campus views here reveal a range of architectural styles as you pass the main gate to the campus at 2.7 miles by the chapel of this oldest-in-America women's institution.

Go by the Congregational Church at 2.9 miles and follow the bends to the north past the college's Skidder Museum. Continue northeast and north on MA 116, soon crossing Leaping Well Brook. Run through a junction with MA 47. Houses thin out at 3.9 miles, and the road meanders through evergreens northeast to Moody Corner in Granby at 4.8 miles. Some mountain views appear ahead as you approach the Holyoke Range at 5.7 miles in more rural country. The range is composed of a long, high, west-to-east upland, about one thousand feet in elevation. Mount Holyoke, itself, on the western end of the range, can be approached from MA 47 and lies in Skinner State Park.

To the right at 7.3 miles, find Holyoke Range State Park and the Robert Frost Trail. You'll see the main entrance to the park a bit farther northward. Frost, perhaps this country's most widely appreciated poet, "a good Greek out of New Hampshire" as he called himself, once lived and taught in nearby Amherst. Crossing the Amherst line and descending in a series of curves, the road levels off by the Atkins Farm and passes the extensive grounds of rural Hampshire College to the left and right, just beyond Bay Road. Some of the college's offices, many in appealing old farmhouses, lie here along 116.

Coming into South Amherst, go over Plum Brook and the Fort River in a farmed lowland, and then into Amherst's residential area. Pass the Hitchcock Center for the Environment and the Commons School, with nice views leftward over ranging fields to the west. MA 116 drops down into the midst of the Amherst College campus once in town, passing the Wilson Admissions Center on Pleasant Street and coming to a tourist information booth near the Mead Art Museum at a crossing where MA 116 and 9 go left at 12 miles. Park at the intersection of Pleasant Street and MA 9 by the green and take an enthusiastically recommended walk around the town center.

Amherst was the lifelong home of the brilliant and reclusive American poet Emily Dickinson, and her residence at 280 Main Street may be visited seasonally. The Jones Library on nearby Amity Street contains notable Dickinson manuscripts and also manuscripts of well-known verse by poet Robert Frost. A visit to the Amherst History Museum at the Strong House on Amity Street provides a glimpse of this community's way of life from the 1700s onward. Richard Sewall's biography, *The Life of Emily Dickinson,* available in local bookstores, offers a picture of both the author and her community.

After a stroll through the campus of Amherst College (founded in 1821), resume this drive by *taking MA 116 and 9 southwest* from the tourist information booth, passing the college field as you head for the point where 116 leaves 9 and runs north again. This brief, inglorious strip west of town is a monument to shopping mall ugliness, but your travel here is, fortunately, short-lived. At 13 miles, *bear right* on 116 north. Here the rural road becomes suddenly a superhighway, the expansive lanes designed to carry traffic north and south *around* Amherst itself—really quite a good idea.

MA 116 gallops north quickly, providing open views to broad fields westward, where tobacco-drying barns are seen. Seldom associated with New England, tobacco has actually long been grown in the Connecticut River Valley in Massachusetts (and even more so in Connecticut). At 15 miles you'll spot continuing vistas to the right of the burgeoning University of Massachusetts campus on the northwest side of Amherst. The skyline is punctuated by the university's numerous high-rise residence halls

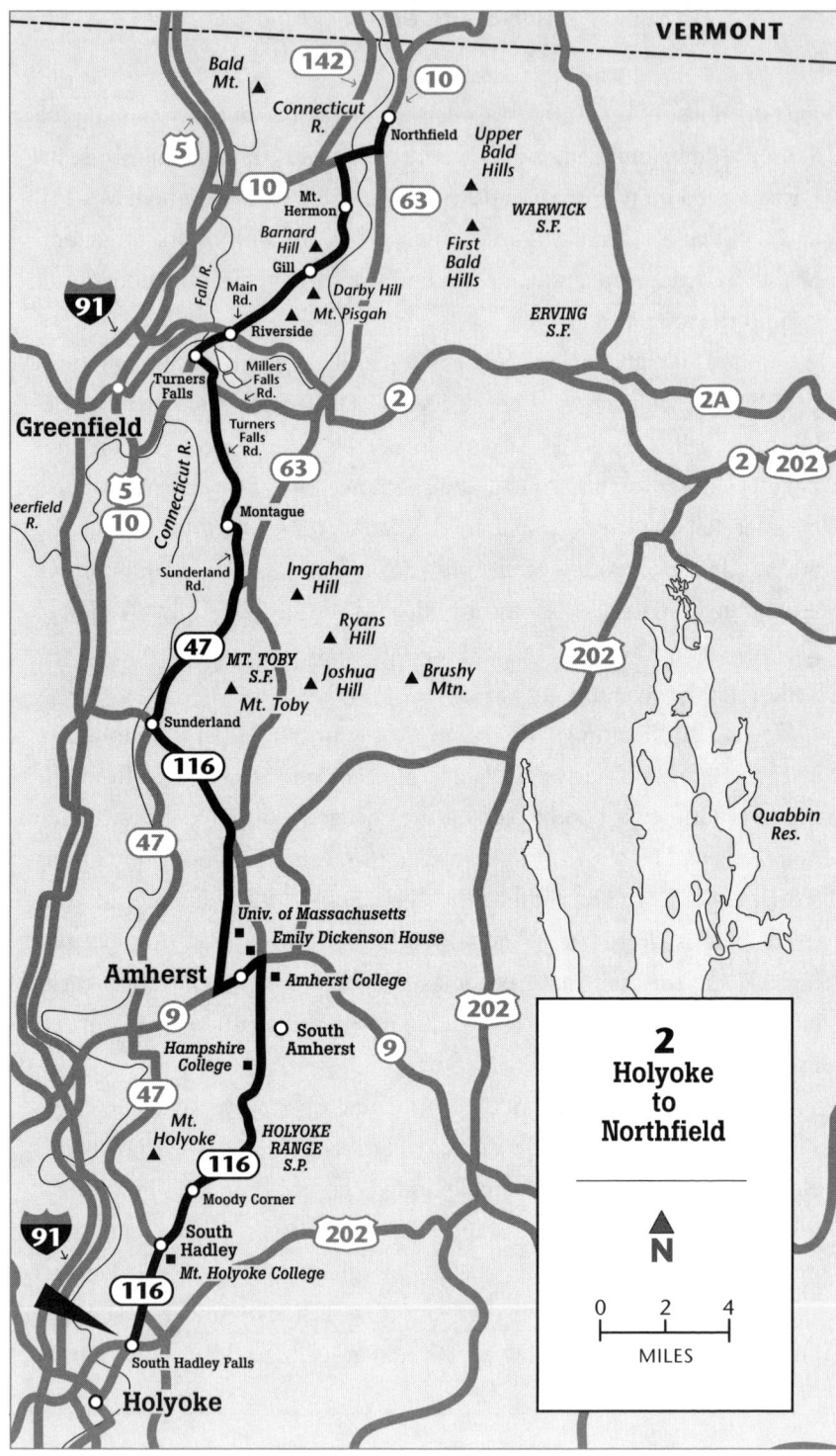

VERMONT

Bald Mt.

(142)

(10)

Connecticut R.

Northfield

Upper Bald Hills

(10)

Mt. Hermon

(63)

WARWICK S.F.

Barnard Hill

Gill

First Bald Hills

(91)

Fall R.

Main Rd.

Darby Hill

Mt. Pisgah

ERVING S.F.

Riverside

Turners Falls

Millers Falls Rd.

Greenfield

Turners Falls Rd.

(2)

(2A)

(5) (10)

(63)

(2) (202)

Deerfield R.

Connecticut R.

Montague

Sunderland Rd.

Ingraham Hill

(202)

(47)

MT. TOBY S.F.

Ryans Hill

Joshua Hill

Brushy Mtn.

Mt. Toby

Sunderland

(116)

(47)

Univ. of Massachusetts

Emily Dickenson House

Amherst

Amherst College

(202)

(9)

Hampshire College

South Amherst

(9)

(47)

Mt. Holyoke

HOLYOKE RANGE S.P.

(116)

Moody Corner

(202)

(91)

South Hadley

(116)

Mt. Holyoke College

South Hadley Falls

Holyoke

2
Holyoke
to
Northfield

N

0   2   4
MILES

and the multistory library. A range of low hills lies off to the north, and an exit and campus-link road are just ahead on the right, if you wish to visit the university grounds.

You cross the Mill River at 16 miles, continuing your ride through more plateau-like, open farm country, gradually pulling around to the northwest in the direction of South Deerfield. This area is actually a broad intervale, its heights, bumps, and wrinkles long ago smoothed by weathering and runoff carried west to the Connecticut River, which is barely a mile and a half to the left now. Go over Russellville Brook at 18.5 miles and cross the Sunderland town line, where the road soon leaves this lovely, open countryside for a very brief dive through more ugly shopping mall congestion. Pass the Sunderland Trout Hatchery in a wooded area as you go over first the Mohawk and then Dry Brooks. Press on northwestward, paralleling a low ridgeline off to the east and reach a state rest area at 20 miles. With the distinctive shape of North Sugarloaf Mountain looming to the west, watch for a junction with MA 47 and *bear right and north* on 47, getting rapidly away from the congestion. You run north now, just a stone's throw from the Connecticut River.

MA 47 goes northward through a neighborhood of older homes and shortly makes its way over more rural ground again. There are hill vistas off to the west as you pass Mount Toby Farm at 22.4 miles. Winding through wooded countryside, the road goes by occasional Connecticut River scenes now. Driving by tilled fields and pasture dotted with cattle, you next cross Gunn Brook and skirt Mount Toby State Forest, where the 1,269-foot mountain of the same name dominates. Farther off to the east lie 1,260-foot Brushy Mountain in Leverett and the collection of lower hills that surround it.

At 25.7 miles you roll over the Montague town line and cross Cranberry Pond Brook. After passing more farms with roadside paddocks, watch for a junction with Sunderland Road at 26.6 miles, where you *leave 47* and *keep left and northwest* for Montague, following the narrow Sawmill River in more quiet backcountry. You drive into Montague center at 27.4 miles, *going left* around the village green and past the post office. Cross the Sawmill River next, taking the Turners Falls Road north. Pass Greenfield Road, cross the railroad tracks at Montague Station, and go by the Massachusetts Fisheries and Wildlife Environmental Law Enforcement Division.

Turners Falls Road proceeds northwest in fields and woods, with Wills Hill to the northeast. At 30.5 miles the road runs through fields for a while and then drops down through a stone cut and embankment, crossing Turnpike Road and then merging with Millers Falls Road. Follow Millers Falls Road into town to a T, where it meets Avenue A, the main street of Turners Falls.

Turners Falls' reason for being is easily apparent if one looks at a map or aerial photograph. The city occupies a peninsula that juts northward into the pathway of the Connecticut River, with the river pooling to the east in attractive Barton Cove. Easterly, beyond the cove, the river has chiseled a broad bend with barlike islands in a place referred to as Deep Hole. Just below, to the southwest, the Deerfield River empties into the Connecticut, and thus fortified, the two race farther south in great, sweeping bends. If ever there was a place to harness waterpower, this is it, as Turners Falls' history as a paper producer and generator of electric power confirms. Of the era of locally generated wealth and manufacturing exuberance, only Avenue A, a stretch of high, bold storefront Victoriana, remains. The downtown merits your on-foot attention, and if you're a confirmed fly fisherman, a shrine of sorts exists here, too. Thomas and Thomas Rodmakers fabricates superb fly rods in its little factory on Avenue A, and visitors are welcomed. The Turners Falls Fish Ladder display off MA 2, open in spring and early summer, is also a fascinating means to observing how waterborne species navigate these rivers.

Go right on Avenue A north as it spans the Connecticut via a high bridge, with excellent views upriver at Barton Cove, and meets MA 2 on the other side. Cross busy Route 2 at 33.8 miles and *go northeast* on Main Road in the direction of Gill. Here you roll northeast in wooded country again between Mason Hill to the left and Pisgah Mountain and Darby Hill to the right. For the time being you are away from and to the west of the Connecticut River. At 35.7 miles, go through the crossroads known as Gill, passing River and Center Cross Roads, and then over Dry and Ashuela Brooks, which run down to the nearby Connecticut. Cattle linger behind stone walls in hillside pastures to the left. Views of more hills appear ahead at Just a Dream Farm as you round Barnard Hill and Stump Mountain to the left in the old Munns Ferry section of Gill. At 37.1 miles, pass Gill Common and Library. You'll find clusters of farm buildings along here, with fine views ranging off to the east. Pull to the north now and enter hilly Mount Hermon in more rural country, with the terrain rising to hillsides on the left. Going over Bailey Brook, soon you emerge at a T with MA 10.

The final leg of this journey requires a *right turn* on MA 10, where you travel east by fields that yield to a vast marsh drained by Bennett Brook and then the Connecticut River, crossed here in one of its wider sections. Once across the big river, you land in the Great Meadows section of Northfield. To the east lie the First and Upper Bald Hills and, behind them, the wild country of the substantial Warwick and Erving State Forests, reached via Maple Street and Gulf Road from Northfield. Erving is the site of the cave home of eccentric hermit John Smith. Smith, who died in 1900, immigrated to the States from the British Isles. Unhappy with the congestion of New York and distressed over the loss of his intended bride, Smith came north. He walked across Massachusetts until he found this hillside cave and determined to live apart, settling in here for thirty years.

Smith fed himself by gathering wild berries, cultivating vegetables, and perhaps hunting. A spring by the cave furnished water, and when he needed money he would take some of his produce and walk toward

Boston to sell it. Before long, he had become famous as the Hermit of Erving Castle, and Bay State gentry climbed up through the woods to visit him, entranced by his eccentricity and fine Scottish brogue. He also conducted hillside religious services, and the wealthy who attended generously left him supplies. A path to the cave has recently been constructed under the direction of naturalist John Foster. Today, Smith lies buried in the Erving Cemetery, a marker for his beloved cat, Toby, beside his grave.

Go left here on MA 63 at 39.2 miles and pull north to the settlement of Northfield. The broad, quiet main street of the community is mostly taken up with the buildings of the Northfield–Mount Hermon School on the right, its attractive campus draped over a low hillside to the east. This drive ends at the school's main gate, at 40.5 miles, less than two miles south of Cheshire County, New Hampshire, and Windham County, Vermont.

The Northfield Mountain Recreational and Environmental Center on Route 63 offers an interesting look at the role of the Connecticut River in the commerce and development of the region. This Northeast Utilities facility pumps river water up the mountain, contains it, and then generates power as water is released through penstocks in a station buried in the mountain. The center features exhibits attesting to the Connecticut's unique contribution to local history.

3

Route
Northampton to Great Barrington
Highway
MA 9, 66, 112, US 20, MA 8, 23
Distance
55 miles

Here is a beckoning drive that zigzags its way through rural countryside
west of the lively college town of Northampton to the little river villages
of Huntington and Otis, up through hill communities such as Monterey,
and on to Great Barrington on the far side of the Berkshires. It's a perfect
escape from things urban and a delightful journey across one of the Bay
State's most rural regions to reach a cultural and recreational hub on the
New York border.

Northampton, the jumping-off point for this excursion, is one of two
major college communities of the "five-college" region. Home to Smith
College, Northampton also attracts students, friends, and families from
Mount Holyoke, Amherst, and Hampshire Colleges and the University of
Massachusetts. With so many students and all that discretionary income
floating around, Northampton has become a town of many restaurants,
cultural venues, and engaging shops. On a summer evening, lines of din-
ers queue to enter popular eateries, people sit and stand along busy Main

Street watching other strolling types, and there seems to be a sort of revelry in the air.

Distinguished modern painters are especially well represented at the Smith College Museum of Art on Elm Street, and the Historic Northampton Museum on Bridge Street offers exhibits on the small city's interesting history, which includes the founding here of the Great Awakening, a 1730s spiritual revival led by local Jonathan Edwards, who was followed, in turn, by the fiery English divine George Wakefield. Both museums are worth exploring before you start your drive to Great Barrington. Occasional performances and concerts at the Academy of Music or Calvin Theater will entertain you, and the artistic fare on view in dozens of local galleries might easily occupy several of your days.

Getting under way, depart the upper square of collegiate Northampton by the "castle," Northampton's fortresslike city hall. *Follow MA 9 west, turning left* onto MA 66 almost immediately after you pass St. Mary's Church. *Go southwest on 66* through the buildings of Smith College, one of that coterie of first-rank women's colleges hereabouts referred to as "the seven sisters." In a mile you'll pass Smith's athletic fields, then move out into more rural turf laced with sumac and hardwoods. Pass the new Hampshire County Jail and House of Correction at 1.6 miles. Cross Lawrence Road at 2.6 miles, where the route winds its way through groves of maple and white pine and enters horse-farm country in paddock-fenced fields as it ascends southwest.

Cross Bassett Brook at 6 miles, and then the Loudville Road, with the Mineral Hills to the north. Eleven-hundred-foot Pomeroy Mountain rises to the left and south as you pass beside the white-fenced pasture at Rolling Gate Farm, and then go by Outlook Farm Orchards at 7.6 miles. Horizon-to-horizon views of the highlands to the west come into sight briefly here. After climbing a little farther westward, the road crests Cub Hill where the Manhan River runs south to hidden White Reservoir.

Loping through a rock cut on this jaunty hill road, you come soon to

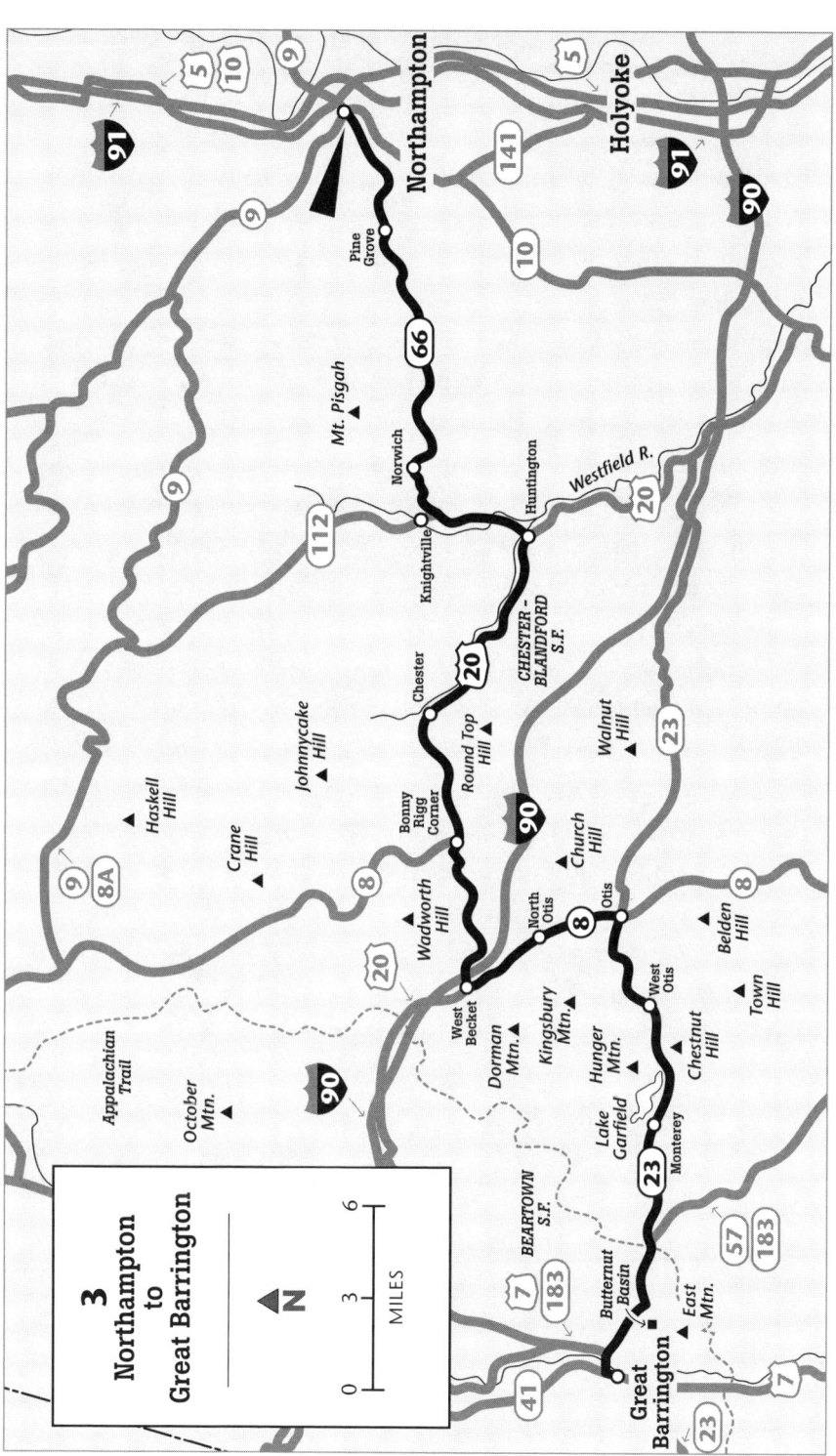

3
Northampton to Great Barrington

MILES

N

0   3   6

the Huntington town line, at 10.7 miles. Just beyond, you're in the tiny hamlet of Norwich, where you descend rapidly with views to the southwest, pass Tucker and Searle Roads, and navigate a rock cut. Follow the marshy bed of Pond Brook now, as both you and it descend through a cleft below Norwich Pond. A challenging 9 percent grade will engage your attention and that of nervous backseat drivers as you wind downward in minutes to a junction with MA 112, *bearing left and south* toward Huntington town center. Here the route follows the meandering, picturesque Westfield River over which there are some pleasing outlooks. You'll pass C. M. Gardner State Park at 14.2 miles with 1,140-foot Deer Hill off to the east. The road crosses the Westfield and then its West Branch as it comes to the center of Huntington beneath little North Rockhouse Mountain.

From Huntington, *go right and west* on MA 20, with railroad tracks and the Westfield River's West Branch to your right as you roll on. The town garnered its name from Charles P. Huntington, who severed a legal Gordian knot locally when he consolidated bits of several townships and two counties into the present community. Earlier, from settlement in the 1760s onward, a couple might be married in one room of a local house only to discover that the marriage was not recognized in other rooms of the same house because the building straddled the boundary between two towns, jurisdictions, or even counties, given the once-prevailing crazy quilt of tangled boundaries here.

Great Morse Hill is to the right as you continue northwest on MA 20, running along the edge of the river on what is called the Jacob's Ladder Trail. It was named after a local wagoneer—Jacob Carter, of Becket—whose team helped many a traveler get over these grades. It's perhaps an appropriate name in its biblical sense, too, given that up ahead lies a summit ridge nearly eighteen hundred feet high, which must have been a worrisome ascent in the horse-and-buggy era. (You'll be able to catch a glimpse of it.) Cross the Chester line at 19.1 miles and come to the

Chester-Blandford State Forest on the left, where campers can find agreeable tenting space and walkers can wander. Hug the side of 1,800-foot Round Top Hill as you run through a shaded cleft at 20.6 miles with mountains rising steeply on all sides. Crossing Griffin Brook you'll have views ahead up a pretty intervale by a bend in the Westfield's West Branch and soon pass the post office in Chester Village, at 23.5 miles. This smallish locality is an informal study in how a community can wrap itself around the course of a dominant river.

At 24.1 miles, go by the Chester Historical Commission at the Old Jail as you climb steeply northwestward, shortly passing the Abbott Memorial, and then pull sharply west, following stony Walker Brook. Pass another campground, and at 25.5 miles the Beckett town line comes in sight and you exit Hampden County for Berkshire County. Becket is a tiny place of fewer than two thousand souls, most having arrived in the last several decades. (The entire original town center disappeared in a roaring flash flood in 1927.) Continue upward through a series of S-curves. Reach open ground and level off, passing a wild bog and arriving at a junction with MA 8 at Bonny Rigg Corners. Climb more, still going westward on MA 20, as the road bends in nearly all directions. At 29.5 miles you'll pass through dense woods.

Finally, you'll descend some, emerging in more open country with fields to the left as you cross Palmer Brook. Pass the entrance to the famous Jacobs Pillow Dance Festival at George Carter Road as you descend farther northwest into a settled area and cross under the Massachusetts Turnpike. (Jacobs Pillow was one of America's first regional dance venues, founded by Ted Shawn in 1932.) Here there are views of hills to the left and an expansive deadwater to your right.

At 33.5 miles from Northampton, you leave MA 20 near an inn and *follow MA 8 left and south* at West Becket. Continue by lovely Shaw Pond, in the embrace of wooded hills on the left, and pass signs admonishing that this is "a winding and dangerous road." You then cross into Otis.

Here, the outflow of Shaw Pond and nearby Cone Brook feeds a lengthy marsh that runs for several miles along both sides of MA 8. The sometimes hidden waterway eventually becomes the West Branch of the Farmington River.

At 38.9 miles, *make a sharp turn right and west* onto MA 23 and pass the Otis Ridge Ski Area, going over Benton and Spectacle Pond Brooks shortly thereafter. To the left and south rises 1,720-foot Filley Mountain. You pass two wild and beautiful extended bogs here through which the two brooks flow. Crossing Tyringham Road at 42.4 miles, you'll see still more bogland to the right, with pleasant views northwest toward Hunger Mountain in Monterey.

The road now drifts southwest, skirting hidden Lake Garfield and crossing the Konkapot River, where distant mountain views appear over paddocks to your right at 45 miles. You descend some to the attractive if diminutive village of Monterey, where you pass the Knox Museum and Library at 45.9 miles. Here also are found the meetinghouse, town hall, and a couple of shops, all on the community's narrow main street. The village, once known as Tyringham, got its start in the 1740s with capital from eastern Massachusetts. Staying south of enormous Beartown State Forest, which is accessible via Brett and Blue Hill Roads on the right just west of town, MA 23 carries you through a junction with MA 183 at 49 miles where it also crosses the Georgia-to-Maine Appalachian National Scenic Trail.

With Warner and East Mountains off to the left, you leave the long stretches of woodland behind now and descend into a more settled region, coming to the Great Barrington town line at just over 50 miles. Go by the entry road to Butternut Basin Ski Area and, at 51 miles, descend again northwest past a 1,400-foot rise on your left known as East Rock, arriving at the junction of US 7 and MA 23 in a couple of minutes. *Go left* at this junction, and drive into the center of Great Barrington on routes 23, 41, and 7. Passing St. Peters Church on the left, head down the pretty, traditional Main Street to conclude this drive at Great Barrington's Town Hall, 55 miles from your starting point in Northampton.

Great Barrington boasts some interesting history. It was the site, in August 1676, of the infamous Talcott Massacre, when a band of Connecticut militia under Major John Talcott slaughtered Indian refugees of King Philip's War who were seeking shelter in New York. Founded in 1766, the town found itself among the earliest communities to test British rule, sacking English circuit-court riders in 1774. Dr. W. E. B. Dubois, founder of the NAACP, was born here, and the town has the unusual distinction of being the first community lit by alternating current after the work of scientist William Stanley shifted the downtown grid from DC to AC in March of 1866.

Great Barrington welcomes travelers today as it did the grandees who flocked here to build the cluster of mansions that characterize the area. Summer brings the Aston Magna Festival at St. James Church, the Stockbridge Chamber Concert series at John Dewey Academy, and, on the northern edge of town, the neighborhood known as Housatonic shelters artists' studios, funky galleries, shops, and eateries of a more contemporary sort. Enjoy!

4

Route
North Adams, Williamstown, Pittsfield, Lenox

Highway
MA 2, US 7, MA 2A

Distance
32.5 miles

Here's a route that captures one of the Bay State's prettiest college towns, what is probably its largest regional cultural center, its highest mountain, and, at the far end, the summer fine-music capital of New England. Along the way there are grand prospects over this northwestern precinct of Massachusetts and farther west to the Taconic Range and New York. And, if you time your journey carefully, you can put your feet up at the end of this trip and take in a live performance by some of the world's great concert artists and orchestras.

North Adams is the stepping-off point for this engaging drive along the westernmost edge of Massachusetts. North Adams is a campus town, home to the Massachusetts College of Liberal Arts (formerly North Adams State College). Once a textile industry hub, electronics manufacturing site, and rail center snuggled up against the Vermont border, North Adams now accommodates the expansive Massachusetts Museum of Contemporary Art (Mass MoCA) cultural center in some of its old mill buildings. Close to town, travelers will find the Western Gateway Heritage Park, focused on the history of the unique Hoosac Tunnel and other railroad memorabilia, and seasonal Natural Bridge State Park, northeast of downtown on MA 8. North Adams's central shopping area has the pleasant flavor of yesteryear right down to a delightful old movie theatre reminiscent of the forties (its screen, unfortunately, now dark).

Begin your trip west and south from North Adams at the intersection of Eagle and Union Streets by the towering spire of St. Francis of Assisi Church opposite St. Joseph's Court. *Drive northwest and west on MA 2*, immediately passing the Massachusetts Museum of Contemporary Art on the right. MoCA is a work-in-progress, its exhibits, displays, studios, and other functions gradually expanding to fill a 250,000-square-foot complex as artists contribute to its growth. With museum partners from all over the country and world, the sprawling former Sprague Electric mill site is on its way to becoming one of the largest contemporary art venues in the country. The cotton looms that long ago occupied these buildings before modern manufacturing arrived have long since gone silent, of course, but current shows, unusual exhibits, resident eateries, and other enterprises make the vast complex live anew.

MA 2 slowly wends its way out of town past several hillside cemeteries in a residential area and, at 1.4 miles, passes Notch Road on the left, which connects with the Mount Greylock summit road. This road, which becomes quite narrow and steep, provides access to the Mount Greylock Reservation and the state's highest mountaintop. One can make the choppy drive to the mountain's summit or walk and explore the numerous trails. At the summit is rustic Bascom Lodge, where limited overnight accommodations are available in season.

The Berkshire region, really more than Berkshire County, is a great, north-south strip down which you are descending. As Kenneth Simpson has observed, "the region is but forty-nine miles long from north to south, extending entirely across the state from Vermont to Connecticut.

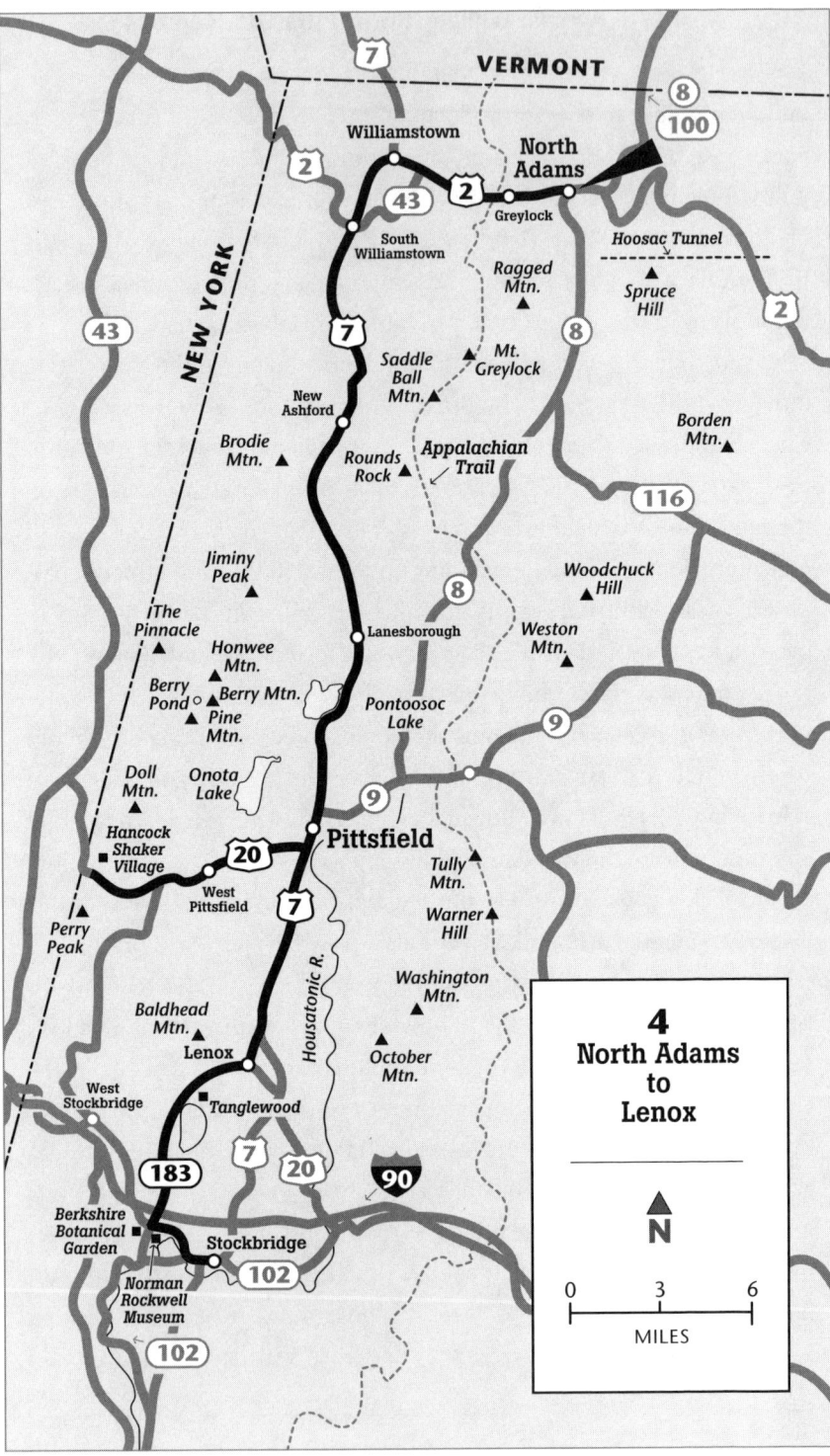

VERMONT

7

8
100

Williamstown

North Adams

2

43

2

Greylock

Ragged Mtn.

Hoosac Tunnel

South Williamstown

Spruce Hill

NEW YORK

7

8

2

43

Saddle Ball Mtn.

Mt. Greylock

New Ashford

Brodie Mtn.

Rounds Rock

Appalachian Trail

Borden Mtn.

116

Jiminy Peak

8

Woodchuck Hill

!The Pinnacle

Honwee Mtn.

Lanesborough

Weston Mtn.

Berry Pond

Berry Mtn.

Pine Mtn.

Pontoosoc Lake

9

Doll Mtn.

Onota Lake

9

Hancock Shaker Village

20

Pittsfield

Tully Mtn.

West Pittsfield

7

Warner Hill

Perry Peak

Housatonic R.

Washington Mtn.

Baldhead Mtn.

Lenox

October Mtn.

West Stockbridge

Tanglewood

183

7

20

90

Berkshire Botanical Garden

Stockbridge

102

Norman Rockwell Museum

102

**4
North Adams
to
Lenox**

N

0   3   6

MILES

 Settler's cottage, Williamstown

In breadth it varies from perhaps twenty-four miles to twelve at its narrowest point. . . . The main topographical features of the region are the Housatonic Valley extending about two-thirds of the way north and south to be continued by the Hoosic Valley, with the Taconic Range to the West, and the Hoosac Range to the east. . . . There are in Berkshire roughly one thousand square miles of forests, attractive fields, hills, rivers and lakes." To confirm Simpson's topology, merely look ahead to the view through your windshield.

Following the Hoosic River, you'll see 2,200-foot Bald Mountain to the right and north with Pine Cobble and East Mountain just beyond. Transit the Williamstown line at 3.5 miles, pull away from the Hoosic, hop cross the Green River at 4.7 miles, and enter a commercial area. Here in Williamstown, you're soon in the midst of the Williams College campus, with the varied and interesting architecture of a school that has been abuilding since 1793 all around you. Both the Williams College Museum of Art and the Sterling and Francine Clark Art Institute are important draws locally. Summer-theater types will take note of the Williamstown Theatre Festival housed in the college's Adams Memorial Theatre, where famous stage and screen alumni return to refresh themselves in summer stock. Williams College's Chapin Library is a haven, too, for those interested in rare books and manuscripts.

Williamstown, a town of about 8,500, was founded in 1765 and took its name from Ephraim Williams, a colonel in the Revolutionary War who commanded Fort Massachusetts and gave his life in skirmishes against the British at Lake George. His bequest to the town of West Hoosac, as Williamstown was then known, provided for the establishment of a school that became Williams College.

On the north side of the college grounds, pass the reconstruction of a typical 1753 settler's cabin and a seasonal tourist information booth next to the Williamstown Inn. *Head left and south* now on US 7 and MA 2, between Bee and Stone Hills. MA 2, the Taconic Trail, departs to the right at 9 miles, heading for Petersburg, New York, through the Taconic Trail State Park. As you proceed south, splendid views of lofty Mount Greylock open up to the left. Buttressed by Mount Williams, Mount Fitch, Stony Ledge, and Mount Prospect, 3,491-foot Greylock carries the Appalachian Scenic Trail northward toward Vermont. The mountain's long, north-south profile is visible for miles here as you roll toward Pittsfield. Grazing cattle and broad fields occupy the foreground, lending this stretch of road an open, almost pastoral feeling.

You reach the New Ashford town line at 12 miles and wind to the south and southwest, moving through a long cleft where there are turnouts for picnicking at 12.5 miles. Cross and recross two arms of the Green River again in this neighborhood, following a lovely intervale. Brodie Mountain Ski Resort is approached at 15 miles. Once a community of farmers, tiny New Ashford now finds its livelihood in the local skiing industry, which, besides Brodie Mountain, includes adjacent Jiminy

Peak. The road next enters Lanesborough, climbing through rock cuts of exposed shale with Sheeps Heaven Mountain, Widow Whites Peak, and Jiminy Peak to the right and west. Drift through a series of S-curves as the road dips southeast to a pretty picnic area on the right at 17.9 miles.

Greylock, Ingraham, and Scott Roads (and, later, North Main Street) connect with the summit road for Mount Greylock along here to the left. Renew your acquaintance with the Green River still again, and then play tag with Town Brook, arriving in 20 miles at the settled section of Lanesborough. Honwee, Berry, and Pine Mountains are the major peaks to the west in Pittsfield State Forest on your right, all seen in the distance behind attractive Pontoosuc Lake at 22 miles. Berry Pond, lodged in these enormous forest lands along the New York state line, claims title to being the Bay State's highest body of water, at 2,150 feet elevation.

You enter Pittsfield while hugging Pontoosuc Lake's east shore, where there is an entrance to a lakeside Rails-to-Trails walking path at 22.5 miles. A side trip on Pecks Road to Berry Pond Road will take you to the high-flung pond of that name, if you're curious. Following US 7, you move through Pittsfield's downtown, passing a junction with MA 9 on your right. Weaponry for the War of 1812 was forged here in the little smithy of Lemuel Pomeroy. Since the 1880s, Pittsfield has been home to dozens of manufactories, some devoted to the plastics industry, with General Electric's plastics division leading the considerable pack. The Living Environmental Concept House on New York Street will introduce you to the latest design concepts in applied plastics technology. As US 7 makes the bend south at the intown Crowne Plaza Hotel, watch for the splendid Berkshire Museum on your left. Take time for a visit here, where artifacts from the Berkshire region's rich cultural history are displayed. The nearby Berkshire Athenaeum also supports exhibits related to Herman Melville. A series of fine buildings line MA 7 as you roll south out of town and pass US 20's point of departure to the west at 26.1 miles.

You may prefer to break off from this route for the short drive *west* be-

A classical moment in Lenox

yond Stearnsville and West Pittsfield on MA 20 to the marvelous Hancock Shaker Village, which keeps alive the important architectural and design elements of the vanishing American Shaker culture. Special programs offered seasonally are of continuing interest in this "City of Peace," as its Shaker inhabitants called it. The 1,000-acre, 20-building complex had its inception in 1790 and now welcomes visitors throughout the year, offering a focal point for modern-day study of Shaker culture.

Going farther southward on US 7, watch for signs now to Arrowhead, the home from 1850 to 1863 of seminal American novelist Herman Melville. The homestead on Holmes Road, managed by the Berkshire County Historical Society, is open to visitors from May to October. Melville composed *Moby Dick* while living here, incongruously landlocked in the great shadow of Mount Greylock for thirteen years.

South of Pittsfield, US 7 finds its way between a range of low mountains on the right and the Housatonic River flowage on the left, backed by the highlands of October Mountain State Forest. At 30.7 miles, West Mountain Road, to the right, will take you to Massachusetts Audubon's Pleasant Valley Wildlife Sanctuary near 1,699-foot Baldhead Mountain. At just over 31 miles, signs for "Historic Lenox" direct you to MA 7A and 183. Leave US 7 and *go right* here, descending into the attractive village center, passing the United Church of Christ and ending this western journey at the Lenox Library Association building at 32.5 miles.

Lenox is indisputably *the* major cultural anchor in the Berkshires. Founded in 1767, the town still reflects the architectural tastes of that panoply of American grandees who made this region a summer watering place in the 1880s. Naumkeag at Prospect Hill, managed by the Trustees of Reservations, is one of the few surviving cottage-mansions open to public view, and surely merits a visit. Long home to the summer concert series of the Boston Symphony Orchestra, Tanglewood is Lenox's biggest musical draw. Open to view is American novelist Edith Wharton's former summer home, the Mount, whose 1902 design and construction Wharton participated in herself. The distinctive residence is illustrative of concepts Wharton had developed in her work, *The Decoration of Houses*. A seasonal Shakespeare series takes place locally, just down the road, and Lenox's Town Hall Theatre offers off-season music with the Armstrong Chamber Concerts series. Inquire locally for an events schedule whenever you visit.

If you can manage time for a stimulating local excursion while in

Lenox, take pleasant MA 183 southwest from town, passing Tanglewood and the Stockbridge Bowl, then following 183 south to its junction with MA 102 where you'll arrive at the striking Berkshire Botanical Garden, and just beyond it, the Norman Rockwell Museum. The 15-acre botanical center features nature trails, specialty gardens, and more than 2,500 plant specimens. The Norman Rockwell Museum, a tribute to the modest man who became America's favorite illustrator, contains a substantial collection of his work and offers conducted tours of his studio and library.

In Stockbridge you'll also discover Chesterwood, the summer residence of famed sculptor Daniel Chester French, who created the Minuteman statue in Concord and the likeness of President Abraham Lincoln in the Lincoln Memorial.

5

Route

BERKSHIRE LOOP:
Pittsfield, Dalton, Cummington,
Plainfield, Savoy, Adams

Highway

MA 9, Plainfield Road, Central Road,
MA 116, 8

Distance

50 miles (around loop)

Here's a tranquil loop running east and then west through the Berkshire Hills. It will carry you through many a small town on quiet back roads. Dividing its time between Berkshire and Hampshire Counties, this route quickly leaves the industrial precincts and baneful shopping malls of Pittsfield for greener ground in Windsor, Cummington, and Plainfield before returning northwest to the towns of Adams, Cheshire, and county namesake Berkshire. Along the way this trip skirts some of the Bay State's larger western state forests, local campgrounds, and state wildlife management areas.

To head for the hills, *go east* in Pittsfield from the junction of MA 9 and US 7, traveling through a series of densely settled residential and business neighborhoods to the junction at 2.8 miles of MA 9 and 8 at

The Most Scenic Roads in Massachusetts

Coltsville five corners. From this tangle of horribly unattractive malls *go east on 8 and 9* toward Dalton. The road widens to an accommodating parkway. Here, you are in the district where famous Crane papers have been made for generations. The Crane Museum is here, too, offering an interesting retrospective on this company and its unique history. The museum's focus lies with the making of paper for currency. All United States paper money is printed on papers made by Crane (and, no, they are not giving away tens and twenties). A bit farther on, you cross the East Branch of the Housatonic River and arrive at the Dalton Post Office in the town center, at 4.6 miles. Now *stay left* on MA 8 and 9 opposite Crane's Westin Mill. There are hills ahead as you pull northeast and play catch with Wahconah Falls Brook in more open country of pastures and scattered woodlands. Baled hay, horses, and silage corn repose in these fields. A side street soon leads to Wahconah Falls State Park, where there are picnicking facilities and a swimming hole by the falls.

At 7.5 miles you'll cross the Windsor town line and climb eastward through several broad curves in wooded countryside, gaining altitude slowly as you ascend to the high ground of the Berkshire Hills. The road stays north of a wide, unsettled region that includes the broken acreage of the Peru Wildlife Management Area. *Continue straight* on MA 9 as 8A goes left and north toward Charlemont at 11 miles, and pass the attractive old Windsor Congregational Church. The road drops southeast now, through dense, pretty hardwood forest dotted with spruce. There are occasional views off to the right. At 12.6 miles you reach a height of land in fine hill country devoid of houses on a road equally devoid of traffic. Mountain views and the shape of a lonely radome lie to the southeast. Soon you will pass High Street Hill on the left, where a short side trip north will take you to Windsor State Forest and camping facilities. Off to the south are the Peru Wildlife Management Area, Middlefield State Forest, and Fox Den Wildlife Management Area. This is the kind of rural country normally associated with territory much farther northward, and

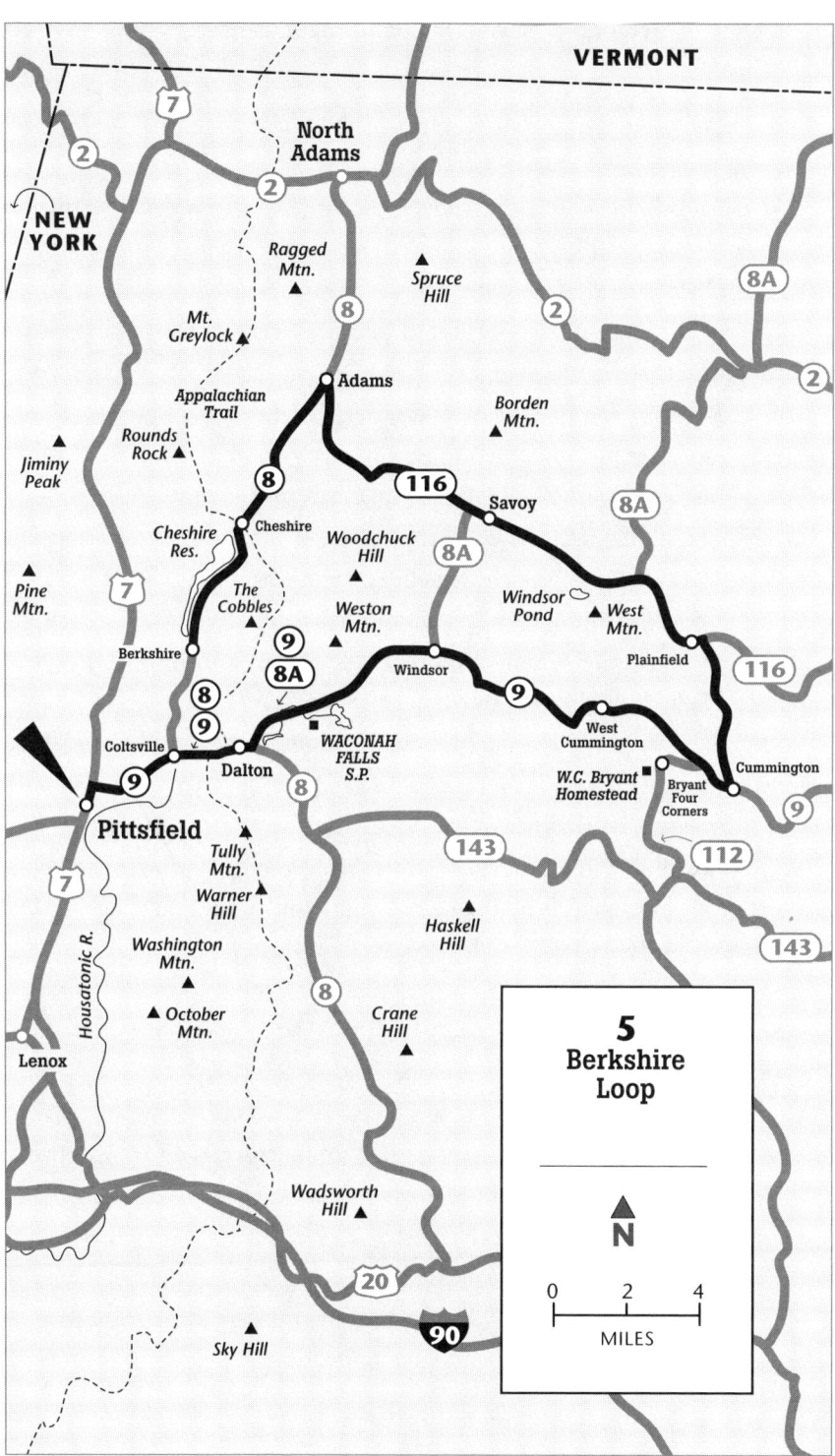

VERMONT

NEW YORK

North Adams

7

2

2

Ragged Mtn.

Spruce Hill

8

8A

Mt. Greylock

Appalachian Trail

Rounds Rock

Adams

116

Borden Mtn.

2

Jiminy Peak

8

Cheshire Res.

Cheshire

Savoy

8A

Woodchuck Hill

8A

Pine Mtn.

7

The Cobbles

Windsor Pond

West Mtn.

Weston Mtn.

Plainfield

116

Berkshire

9

8A

Windsor

9

8

9

West Cummington

Cummington

Coltsville

Dalton

WACONAH FALLS S.P.

W.C. Bryant Homestead

Bryant Four Corners

9

9

7

Pittsfield

8

Tully Mtn.

143

112

Warner Hill

Housatonic R.

Washington Mtn.

Haskell Hill

143

October Mtn.

8

Lenox

Crane Hill

5 Berkshire Loop

▲ N

Wadsworth Hill

0   2   4
MILES

20

90

Sky Hill

it can come as a surprise to those who think of Massachusetts as being everywhere densely settled.

Descend southeast and then pull abruptly north as you follow hidden Westfield Brook, which you cross in minutes. Roll east again along the Westfield River in a series of tight turns. The road, slabbing along a hillside, cuts through uplands here and brings you to nice river outlooks through the trees at 18.2 miles. Cross the river again where there are several riverside turnouts above the water. Go through a junction with MA 112 south at just under 21 miles, and enter Cummington. This quiet little community was once home to American poet, orator, and lecturer William Cullen Bryant, whose *Thanatopsis* had local inspiration. Bryant so loved this western Massachusetts hill country that he returned here for a part of each year until he was well into his eighties. The Bryant homestead, on the West Cummington Road at its intersection with MA 112, is open to view during the summer.

Watch carefully here for the spot on the immediate *left* just beyond the junction with 112 where you *turn northeast* off MA 9. Make this turn and *go left again* immediately onto Plainfield Road. You cross the Westfield River once more on a distinctive little bridge. Take narrow Plainfield Road north just west of the Franklin County line, where there are some nice views westward, at 22 miles, from a high ridge.

Plainfield Road becomes Central Road as it climbs north and curves past a sugarhouse into high fields with excellent views on both sides. Hard rock (sugar) maples border the road where there are views over your shoulder to the southeast. Just beyond here, I've slowed to allow whole flocks of wild turkeys to cross this thoroughfare after they've had their lunch in an apple orchard to the right. More grand maples stand like sentries along this street near the Thatcher Farm. At 25 miles you'll crest the hill in open pasture at Back Acres Farm. Passing through additional elegant stands of maple, you'll begin to enter a built-up area as you reach the center of Plainfield.

At 25.6 miles, you arrive in the quiet, appealing crossroads that is Plainfield and *bear left* on MA 116 by the Hudson House Memorial School, Shaw Memorial Library, and Hathaway Hall. Head west with excellent views left and right in this village of older houses, and pass the Plainfield Town Hall on the right with still more views to the western ridgeline. North Union Street on the right leads to Kenneth Dubuque Memorial Forest. MA 116 is lined with hard rock maples and old stone walls as it runs through an intervale to the northwest now in very rural terrain with lovely woods and pasture outlooks backed by mountains. Pass a junction with MA 8A at 28.1 miles; 8A north leads to additional access routes to the Memorial Forest and Stump Sprouts Cross-Country Ski Center.

Continue west on MA 116 and 8A, rolling by attractive Plainfield Pond, where there are turnouts and a boat-launch facility. Shortly you enter Berkshire County. A connector road to the left along here runs by hidden Windsor Pond to camping facilities at nearby Windsor State Forest. (Hikers in the state forest will find the gorgelike Windsor Jambs worth exploring.) Climb next past a rangy deadwater and by a campground at 28.7 miles. A minute or so farther on you enter the township of Savoy. Drive by a line of pretty older houses and dip northwest as you go past a second access road on the left to Windsor State Park's campground. At 32.8 miles you'll descend into the village of Savoy, where you pass the Baptist Church and Center Road. Center Road runs northward to Savoy Mountain State Forest, where there are further opportunities for camping near North Pond and a fine network of hiking trails that will take you to, among other places, the bold summit of the nearly 2,600-foot Spruce Mountain. Center Road also climbs through Savoy Center, where a local side street will carry you to the top of 2,500-foot Borden Mountain. Ask locally also for directions to Tannery Falls, a pretty drop in confluent Ross and Parker Brooks.

From Savoy westward, the route runs around the south end of the

Hoosac Range. There are good views leftward from this high ground at 33.9 miles. Further outlooks toward towering Mount Greylock appear to the northwest as you descend into Cheshire township, passing the handsome Gulf Farm at Stewart White Road. A winding descent follows as one drops into the cleft between the ranges, and you'll be able to gaze well off to the southwest as you drop down into the residential area. Cross Dry Brook and pass local Hoosac Valley schools, going north through Arnoldsville into the center of Adams. At 40 miles there are occasional river views leftward beneath the bold rockslides on Mount Greylock's east side. Just beyond, you arrive at a junction with MA 8 in Adams by St. Mark's Episcopal Church.

Go left and south on MA 8, proceeding through the center of Adams, where there are some interesting views of the big mountain despite this being a settled residential and business area. In McKinley Square, watch for a memorial to President William McKinley, an honored friend of the substantial textile manufacturing industry that once thrived here. Incorporated in 1778, Adams took its name from revolutionary patriot Samuel Adams and owed its existence to a group of agriculturally minded Quakers who farmed hereabouts. Suffragette Susan B. Anthony was born in Adams, too. The community gradually became a manufacturing center, giving birth to mill machinery, paper, and plastics industries.

You bridge Dry Brook again and, in more open countryside at 42.6 miles, enter the built-up center of Cheshire. The road slabs the hillside and climbs south and southwest, with views toward Cole Mountain on the right and an 1,850-foot formation known as The Cobbles on the left. You cross the Appalachian National Scenic Trail here, too, as it goes through town, headed west and then north for its lengthy traverse of Mount Greylock. Pass the Massachusetts State Police Cheshire barracks at a height of land at 43.3 miles and continue south in rolling countryside with occasional outlooks south and southeast.

Though you are still surrounded by hills, the last miles of this drive become increasingly developed and commercial. An exception is the attractive Cheshire Reservoir on the right at about 46 miles. MA 8 follows this long, north-south body of water for some distance. Along an old railroad bed a Rails-to-Trails path has been created that offers some pleasant strolling beside the water. The lake is backed by Rounds Rock and Savage Hill. At 47.5 miles, North and Weston Mountains in the Chalet Wildlife Management Area are visible to the left and east. The road runs through more open farm country at 48.2 miles, where roadside stands brim with thousands of pumpkins in the autumn. With Laurel and Constitution Hills to the west, cross into Lanesborough at 49.1 miles and conclude this circuitous drive at just under 50 miles, in the little community that takes its name from both the county and the hills that rise around it to eastward. ✒

6

Route
Around Quabbin Reservoir

Highway
MA 2A, 32, 9, US 202

Distance
62 miles

Quabbin's north-south dimensions fill about one-third of the state when looked at from above, making it the largest body of water in Massachusetts. The expansive Quabbin reservation, which is so large it resides in three counties, nestles like a living heart in the center of the state, a reminder of the earth and water on which we all depend for our very existence. This highly valued source of potable water and the more than 81,000-acre protected woodland that surrounds it are home to many bird and animal species. Across the road from the reservation lie the small, pretty towns and faded little industrial enclaves that once tied this region to the Bay State's version of the Industrial Revolution. A drive around Quabbin is both a trip through the country and a revisiting of a style of life that is rapidly passing away.

To make the journey around Quabbin, leave the Memorial Building and police headquarters in downtown Athol, a small manufacturing city in north central Massachusetts. Athol can be reached easily from east or west via MA 2 and 2A. *Go east* over a steel bridge on MA 2A and 32 above the rail line and rows of brick factory buildings that still convey this city's industrial attachments. Rising through a residential area, pass the Athol Grange, the Athol Historical Society, and soon go by the Thurston Conservation Area on the left.

At 1.3 miles you pass the Massachusetts State Police barracks and *keep right* on MA 32, going south near hidden Lake Ellis. You continue south and southeast here, going under US 202 and MA 2 at 2.3 miles, and then along a lengthy stretch of marshy woods to the right, fed by outflow from Lake Ellis. The road climbs some through spare, rural countryside by 3.7 miles and crosses into Petersham. Here you soon roll over Nelson Brook, which connects to the west with Riceville Pond in Petersham State Forest. Here, too, at just under 4 miles, you come to the Fisher Museum of Harvard Forest, one of the great private woodland holdings in the Bay State. The Harvard Forest lands will flank the left side of the road for miles. Past the Petersham Country Club, at 6 miles, are low stone walls and a series of fine old colonial homes. Views eastward to adjacent ridgelines become visible as this route follows a high ridge.

At 7.4 miles you go through a junction with MA 101 and descend through some rolling green pasture screened by roadside trees. At St. Peters Church, pull more to the southwest and then come to the Petersham Craft Center at 7.9 miles. Now you drift into Petersham village itself, where it's worthwhile to pause and enjoy the brilliant, wide common backed by old Federal and Greek Revival houses and the stately Unitarian church. That ubiquitous New England civic institution, the bandstand, sits on the common, and opposite are the town hall and library. A sunny autumn afternoon here conjures up the life of typical New England small towns in another era, an effect quite pleasant and easy on the eyes.

Continue south on 32 and 122 to Barre, winding southeast and south through hardwood forest lined with stone walls. Still more Harvard Forest lands lie to the left. The road parallels lowlands fed by Moccasin

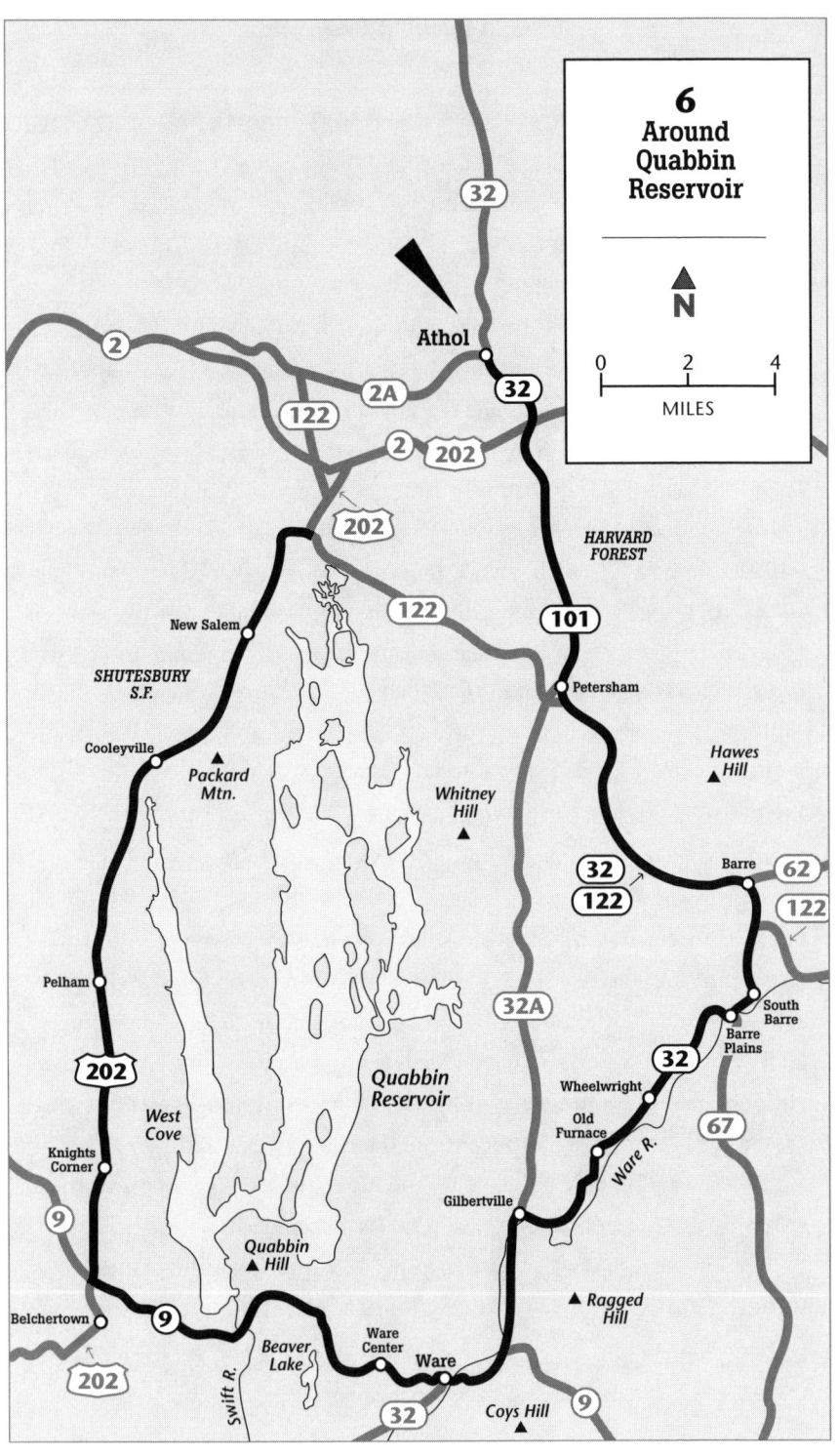

6
Around Quabbin Reservoir

N

0   2   4
MILES

Brook, with views to hills ahead to the southeast. Pass a little pond to the left and cross the East Branch of the rocky Swift River. Now you roll in a more easterly direction above Moose Brook Wildlife Management Area, at 10.8 miles. Passing groves of white pines and birches, go through a rocky cut at 12.1 miles and climb south toward Barre center. Go by a bogland dense with dead standing trees and descend here.

Some views to the west appear at 13.9 miles, and you pass an inn, arriving at the pretty Barre town common at 15.9 miles. A number of interesting older houses line the village center. *Keep right* by the Barre Players Theatre, and from the *east* side of the grassy common *take MA 32 and 122 south* through a section of traditional homes, farms, and horse paddocks. Drift southeast now, crossing and following Galloway Brook, where stone walls occasionally border the road. Keep south on MA 32 when 122 departs eastward. At 18.1 miles, in rural surroundings, you come to a connector road to Pine Ridge Ski Area.

You're on your way here through a cluster of ghostly old industrial buildings reminiscent of commercially better days hereabouts. Cross the Ware River in South Barre, where you pass the post office at 19.2 miles. Go southwest on 32 next to the Barre Plains, recrossing the Ware River and following its marshy outflow to the left into Wheelwright. You jump Pine Hill Brook and roll over the Hardwick town line at 21.4 miles, and then pass open fields and several attractive ponds, which are links in the continuing Ware River marshlands. Here you also come to a connector road to Winimusett Wildlife Management Area and go through a neighborhood known as Old Furnace, with ridgeline views to westward over cornfields. Cross a rail line at 22.6 miles and come to the Wheelwright Art Center with further outlooks over the Ware River marshes to the left and southeast.

Still trending southwestward in this progression of little communities divided by rolling hills and streams, go by the road to Hardwick center on the right at 23.7 miles, dropping toward the Gilbertville section of

Hardwick, where MA 32 and 32A join. Follow the omnipresent Ware River through Wheelwright and gain a little altitude now, leaving the river valley for some splendid vistas south and southwest at 24.5 miles near 1,200-foot Ragged Hill. The route straddles the Hampshire and Worcester county lines here with pleasant views eastward. Descend on a straight stretch of road running southwest and west with hill outlooks ahead and to the left.

Next you'll enter the reclusive little community of Gilbertville at 27.5 miles, *keeping left and south* and going by some abandoned mills and crossing a railroad line. A town once organized around manufacturing, Gilbertville still possesses rows of old mill housing that you see on the right as the road turns toward Ware, still following the Ware River into Hampshire County. The river widens to a broader marsh near open fields backed by ridgelines as you cross the New Braintree town line at 28.8 miles and the Ware town line just beyond. Here the river takes the form of two attractive ponds to the right. Just beyond, MA 9 joins 32, and the two run together into the center of Ware at 31.6 miles. This is the south-ernmost point in this drive around Quabbin, views of which you'll have before long.

Staying with MA 32 and 9 now, go under a rail line and cross Muddy Brook. You'll see some hill scenes off to the southeast. Appealing old mills here have been converted to modern uses. *Follow 9 right and northwest* as it leaves 32, and look left for some excellent distant outlooks at 33.3 miles. There continue to be good views over rolling countryside to the west as you drive through Ware Center, pass the 1742 Congregational meetinghouse, and approach the first of several access points for visiting Quabbin Reservoir (watch for signs).

Take time to visit the reservoir's shores via this entrance or, farther on, at the Windsor Dam site in Belchertown. This vast body of water had its birth in 1927, after years of courthouse wrangling over the Common-wealth's attempt to dam the Swift River and flood this valley. Four entire

 On the green at Petersham

towns were evacuated and now lie underwater. The Swift very slowly filled this low-lying basin, and the reservoir reached its capacity in 1946. Creation of the Quabbin Reservoir was (and still is) seen by a few as a cruel imposition on the Bay State's rural center in order to provide water for flushing toilets in distant Boston.

Just beyond the Beaver Lake deadwater, the Old Ware–Enfield Road leads to the right in West Ware over 1,026-foot Quabbin Hill. In stands of uniform red pines you proceed along the Covey Wildlife Management Area (left) and reach the entrance to Quabbin Park at 38.4 miles, by the Swift River. If you didn't stop at the entrance mentioned earlier, be sure to visit the reservoir and dam at this point and see firsthand the enormous body of water you have been circling. There are picnic and hiking facilities here, and in the Metropolitan District Commission Building next to the dam you'll find a sort of historical museum capturing the story of Quabbin's development. Massachusetts Wildlife Field Headquarters also are seen on the left in this section of MA 9 at 39.1 miles.

Crossing Jabish Brook, *turn right and north* on US 202 at 42.7 miles, making the long, uninterrupted climb up the ridgeline of 1,115-foot East Hill. You continue alongside Jabish Brook to the north where it mingles with tiny Knights Pond. Rising through the countryside of Belchertown, the road runs through hundreds of acres of rural hardwoods, now with very few houses. Good easterly views appear to rightward at 44.2 miles from your starting point. Lands visible to the right are almost entirely part of the Quabbin reservation.

Roll across the Pelham town line at 46.1 miles as you near the north-westernmost portion of this loop. You're presently traveling above Quabbin's narrow, hidden West Cove, which is set off from the main body of water by the Prescott Peninsula. Pelham was once the home of Daniel Shays, who in 1786 led an uprising (the Shays Rebellion) against taxation and confiscation of farmers' lands. Having fought to rid themselves of the yoke of British oppression, Shays and his followers refused to quietly submit to the new tyranny of a tax-happy Massachusetts General Court. Long live Daniel Shays!

As you go through the Knight's Corner section of Pelham, a marshy lowland can be seen to eastward, screened by forest. Like much of this west side of the reservation, the area appears wild and unspoiled. Hidden from the eye is wooded Mount Lincoln, a 1,238-foot summit just to the west and left in red- and white-pine forest. You are almost that high as you drive northward here, a measure of how much the road has climbed since leaving the Ware River drainage.

Pass Amherst Road at 50.1 miles and watch carefully for beautiful glimpses of the valleys and ranges to the east, on your right. A stone-walled turnout offers a place to park. Cross into Shutesbury, in Franklin County, still well up in this high country. Go over the West Branch of the

Swift River and next through a neighborhood known as Cooleyville as US 202 pulls more generally to the northeast. You will pass a connector road on the left to Shutesbury State Forest shortly. In a few minutes more, you cross Hop Brook and travel through New Salem.

The route next begins to descend northwest of Rattlesnake Hill and passes the Rattlesnake Hill Gate to Quabbin Reservoir (another point of access) just before MA 122 comes in on the right. Lower now, the route runs over the boggy drainage of the Middle Branch of the Swift River and to a junction with MA 122, where this drive ends. To head farther west, north, or east, follow MA 202 another mile and a half to connections with MA 2. 🏃

7

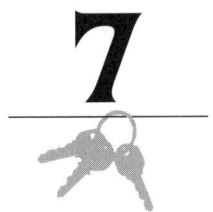

Route
Great Barrington, South Egremont to
Mount Washington State Forest
Highway
US 7, MA 41, Mount Washington Road,
East Street, Cross Road
Distance
29 Miles (round trip)

Here is a short drive out and back, taking in one of the most fascinating hidden corners of the Bay State—a special mountainous nook and cranny little seen by most travelers who pass through the better-known, bustling resort towns that lie nearby. At the end of this route you'll find a serene, undisturbed woodland shaped by surrounding mountains, all wrapped around a great, deep chasm that's home to a waterfall of striking beauty. About as far as you can get from big-city versions of Massachusetts, this drive takes you to a wild pocket of state forest upland hard against the New York state border.

Begin in the center of Great Barrington and *take US 7 south* through the Berkshire Heights section of town in the direction of Great Barrington Airport. This busy parkway shortly brings you to the junction of US 7 with MA 41 and 23, where you *go right and southwest* on 41 opposite

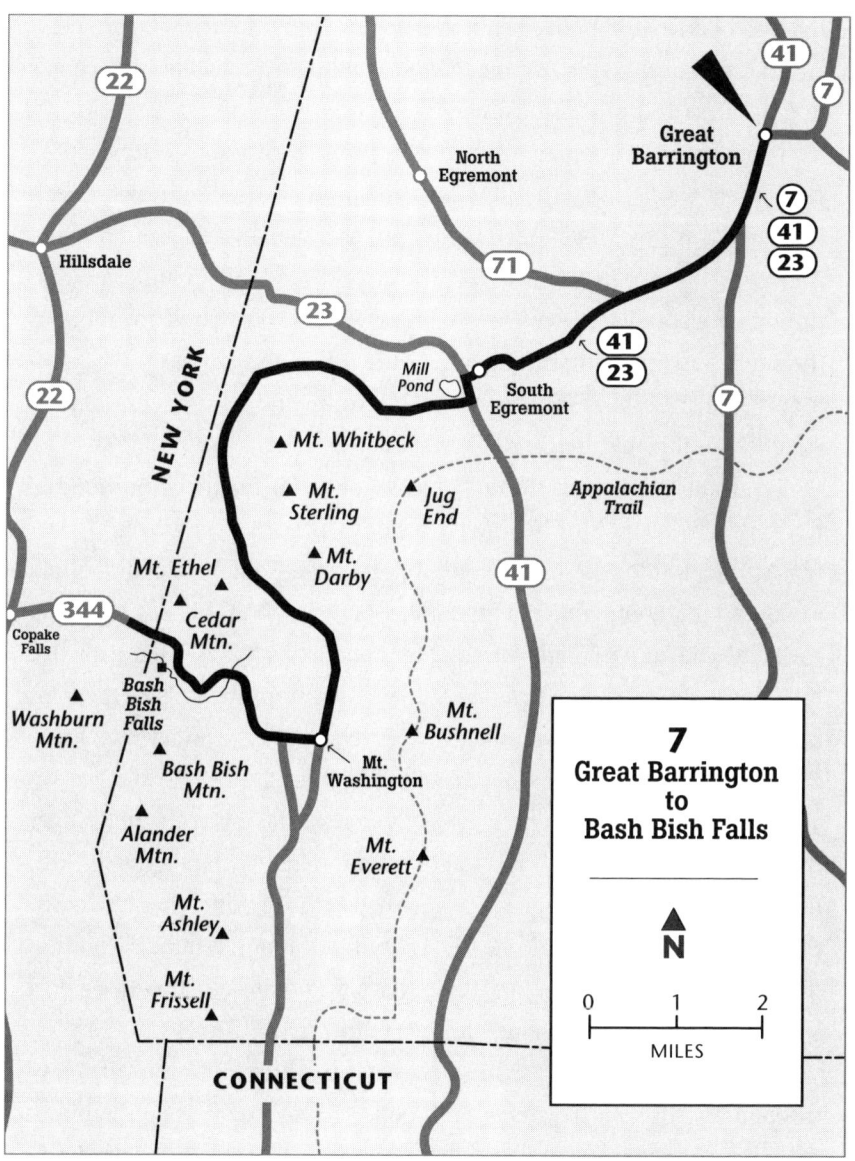

the Great Barrington police headquarters. Set your odometer to zero here. Go southwest on Maple Avenue (MA 41) and pass a rehabilitation center in a business and professional neighborhood.

There are rewarding views before you to the west and southwest. At just under a mile from the junction, you'll cross the diminutive Green River and drive by broad, open fields with occasional views around to the northwest. You soon pass MA 71, the airport road, at 1.2 miles and go through a glade dotted with white pines. At 2.8 miles you turn more to the southwest, crossing the Egremont town line and going by the Egremont Country Club. You are still on routes 23 and 41, which companionably run together here.

The route now winds through a series of bends in a neighborhood of fine old houses and inns in a pretty historic district where groves of Norway spruce border the road. Going by the First Congregational Church in South Egremont, you come to a junction where MA 23 goes right and west and you *keep left and south* by Mill Pond at 3.6 miles. This attractive little body of water is part of a long marsh fed from the hills to the west by Kenner Brook, and is seasonally host to a variety of waterfowl, especially Canada geese. You *go immediately right* around the pond at 3.8 miles and travel Mount Washington Road due west, staying with the Kenner Brook flowage. The marsh lies to your right, dense with tall grasses, cattails, and alder, offering open views to the north. To your left are two distinct summits: Jug End and nearly 1,800-foot Mount Whitbeck, both in the Jug End State Reservation. If you peer over your left shoulder, you'll see 1,800-foot Mount Bushnell to the southeast.

Pass Jug End Road at 5.5 miles, beyond pastures off to the left. Drive through a sparsely settled neighborhood, and say goodbye to the bright lights as you begin to climb steadily. Skirting the rangy flanks of Mount Whitbeck, you turn southward, ascending into Mount Washington State Forest at 7.3 miles. There are some excellent outlooks to the left toward Mount Sterling and Mount Darby as you rise along tilted ledges of metamorphic rock. Through dense hardwoods you can occasionally glimpse solid Mount Everett, the highest peak in the region, off to the southeast. You sail along blissfully here, nearly nineteen hundred feet in the air and just below the summit of Prospect Hill, which lies through the woods to your right. A few houses appear and disappear in mixed-growth forest as you proceed south on what is now called East Street.

Overarching trees spread canopy-like above the road, forming a sensuous green tent in summer, and low stone walls set a pretty border to the woods as the road turns southeastward at 8.7 miles. You pass a stately old farmhouse, cross Guilder Brook, and come to the entrance road to Mount Everett State Reservation at 11.2 miles. (In the warmer months, you may wish to make a side trip here on a narrow road that ascends the 2,600-foot mountain.) Continuing southward on East Street, in a few hundred yards you'll need to slow down as you go by the Mount Washington Town Offices and the Church of Christ, *bearing right and west* on Cross Road.

Buckle up and keep eyes forward as you next descend west on a winding 15-mph course through fern-choked woodlands that takes you down Larch Hill and around a hairpin curve to the banks of Wright Brook. As the sign indicates, this very slender road will carry you to New York state. Go southwest at a leisurely clip along Wright Brook, where several turnouts make it possible to pause and enjoy the superb river views. The brook gradually disappears in a deep chasm as you pull west and then northwest and soon begin following Bash Bish Brook along Falls Road. A last, lonely house is passed. This deep cleft between Cedar and Bash Bish Mountains provides a continuous natural feast for the eye whenever you visit—heady in spring, spellbinding in autumn. At 13.8 miles, the road gets down to river level briefly and then tilts and narrows. (You know you're in unusual terrain when the road tilts too much for crews to paint a yellow line down the middle of the right-of-way.) Indeed, the centerline ends abruptly, and you climb around a bend to the parking area at Bash

Bash Bish Falls, Mount Washington

Bish Falls at 14.5 miles, in the midst of 4,500 acres of serene natural woodlands.

These striking Mount Washington State Forest grounds are dominated by groves of tall hemlocks, which shelter a marked trail that descends in about a quarter-mile to spectacular Bash Bish Falls. The walk is a must, and for your effort you'll be well rewarded with close-up views of the falls, a cataract that plunges over a series of cliffs and into the westward-running brook of the same name. The falls are most impressive during the March/April runoff. This is an immensely attractive and peaceful place, a bit of nature well preserved and defended against development. The scene reminds one inevitably of wilderness explorer and naturalist John Muir's statement: "There is nothing more eloquent in Nature than a mountain stream."

If you're determined to cross into New York and see these falls from the New York side, continue westward beyond the parking area on the paved road, which becomes NY 344 in less than a mile. A view of the lower falls and access to hiking trails are in the Taconic State Park, below to the west.

Haydn Mason has recounted the Indian legend of Bash Bish, the mother-goddess of the falls. She gave birth, it is said, to a beautiful child who would be named White Swan by the Black Thunder tribe who found and adopted her. In time, she was married to Whirling Wind, son of the tribal chief. Her beauty and her faithfulness were legendary, but White Swan could not bear her brave a son. He took a second, more human wife, as was the custom in such cases. In her despair at being replaced, White Swan rushed to the great capstone of the falls one moonlit night and called to her mother to take her back. She leapt into the mists and was embraced by her mother, never to be seen again.

Beyond the falls, the nearest communities on the New York side are Copake Falls and Hillsdale. To return to Great Barrington, retrace your route east and north, remembering to turn left at the church at East Street in the village of Mt. Washington. The brooks and enchanting, woodsy cover along this drive offer surprising new delights to the eye on the return. The round trip, out and back, is a relaxed 29 miles.

Note: A little reminder, not in the least intended to frighten you. This is one of those very few places in western Massachusetts where, very rarely, venomous snakes may be present. Little pockets of copperheads and the even rarer timber rattler are reported to exist in rocky cover in these extreme western hills. There is much disagreement among scientists about which species occur, and where and in what numbers. Some believe the sightings are aberrations and that the area is really too far north of their normal range for these reptiles to be a concern, but the fact remains that a few individuals or dens have been seen here. Since I enjoy getting out of the car and walking along the streams and paths of this outstandingly beautiful countryside, I sometimes have to remind myself to keep my eyes and ears open as I step through brushy, leafy terrain exposed to the warmth of the sun. You should do the same when in this neighborhood, especially keeping your eye on any youngsters traveling with you. The danger is very small, but worth avoiding.

8

Route
Westfield to Dalton

Highway
US 20, MA 112, 143, 8

Distance
43.1 miles

This route climbs across the rural western third of the Bay State from Westfield, near Springfield, to the pleasant town of Dalton, just east of Pittsfield. Rising through wooded hill country, the drive follows a major river northwestward and then lopes through the 2,000-foot-high uplands of the Berkshire Range, delivering you to the center of regional cultural and recreational activities along the Massachusetts border with New York state. The route negotiates high, wooded, undeveloped backcountry that is blissfully free of traffic, a perfect antidote to baneful urban motoring.

The drive begins at the junction of US 20 with MA 10 and US 202 in the heart of Westfield. (This point can be reached via Mass Turnpike Exit 3. From Exit 3 take MA 10 and US 202 south to the junction with US 20.) US 20 winds west out of town in a built-up area, passing the First Battalion, 104th Infantry Armory on the right in a half mile. At 3.2 miles west of the junction, you begin to enjoy views of the hardy Westfield

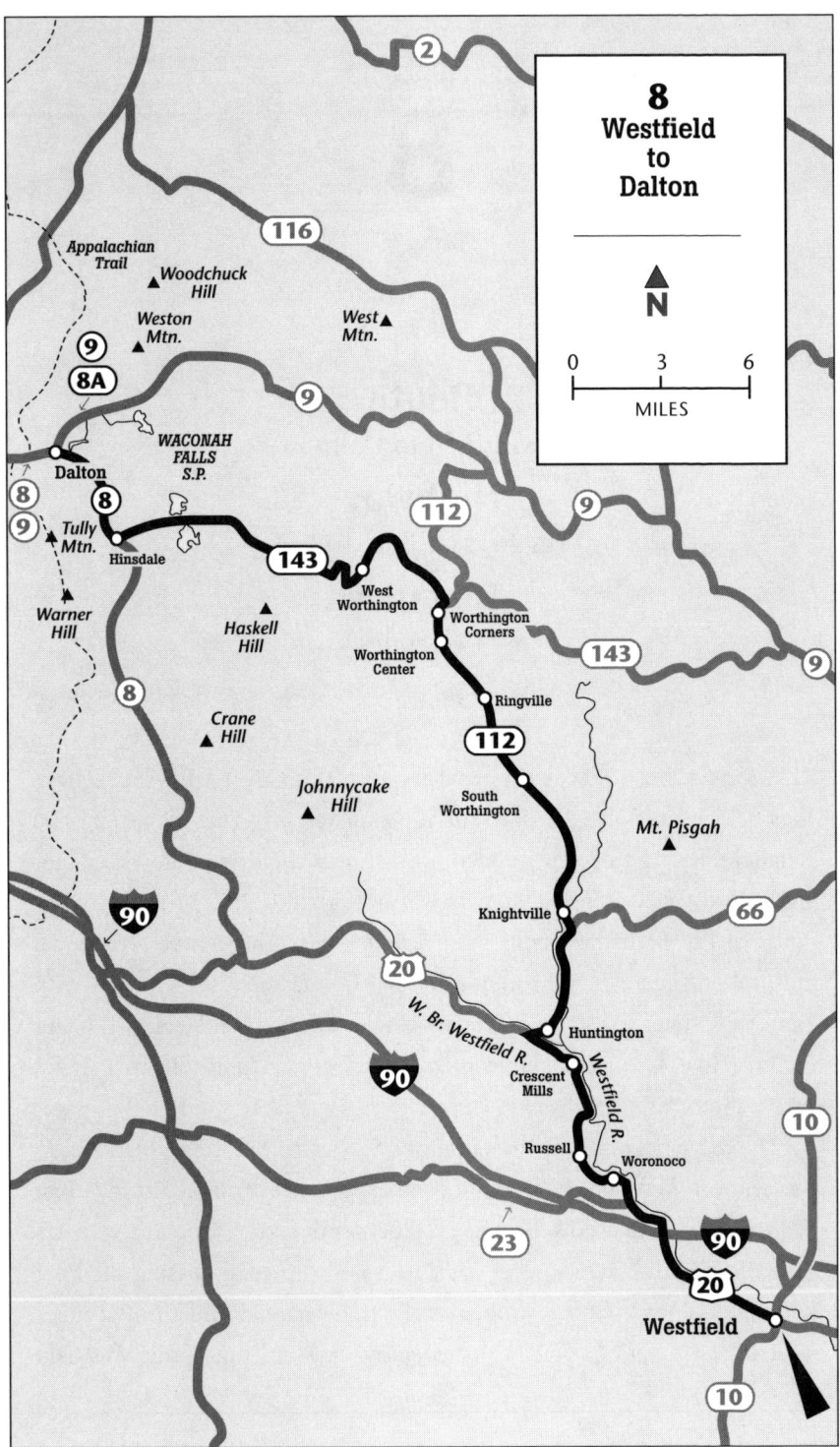

8
Westfield
to
Dalton

N

0   3   6

MILES

River, which you will follow north off and on all the way to Huntington. Just beyond, on the right, you will find a river access point.

You leave Westfield and enter Russell at 4.4 miles, getting out into more rural, leafy countryside. Thousand-foot-high Russell Mountain stands to the left as you go under US 90, hugging the Westfield River. There are some fine exposed ledges to the east and northeast in this section. Come next to the first entrance road to Strathmore Paper's Woronoco Mill site where you'll have additional outlooks over those ledges.

Go through a junction with MA 23 shortly, where you *keep right and north* on US 20 and pass, at 5.2 miles, another access road to the Woronoco Mill. Look for broad cliffs above the river to the east. North of the mill, the road pulls away from the river a bit, skirting Punchbowl Mountain on the left, then reconnecting with the water again as it comes into the center of Russell. You pass the Massachusetts State Police barracks in Russell at 8 miles. Beyond Russell center the route again hugs the Westfield River in pretty Pioneer Valley countryside, rising to Crescent Mills at just under 11 miles. You'll cross into Hampshire County here, making a bend parallel to the river and going northwest. Drive through a couple of rock cuts with retaining walls and then into the settled area of Huntington.

Huntington is the starting point for the Westfield River Wildwater Canoe Races each April. If you visit here during race weekend, you'll find that the runs on the rough-and-ready river are quite a spectacle. The Westfield loses its quiet demeanor when the river is choked with runoff, and the canoe ride southward is not for the faint of heart at such moments. In Huntington, you will *leave US 20* and cross the railroad tracks and West Branch of the Westfield River as you *go right* onto MA 112.

The route now drifts north through some low, boggy woodlands and past a series of turnouts where there are several outlooks above the water. North Rockhouse Mountain is over your right shoulder to the southeast. Cross the Westfield at Norwich Bridge at 13.4 miles just below where the waterway divides. The river's middle branch comes in from the north-west via Littleville Lake in what is known as Goss Heights. (To explore this pretty area more thoroughly, take local roads to the Littleville Lake Project on the left.)

You come to C. M. Gardner State Park at 14.8 miles, and then will wind by some excellent views of rocky river rapids and pass a junction with MA 66. You'll cross Pond Brook, the Westfield River, and Sykes Brook (now in Knightville), and climb northwest and north. An entrance to the Knightville Dam Project is on your right shortly, where there are some spectacular water views at 17 miles and opportunities for boating and wildlife observation. A height of land is reached beyond the dam, and you ascend through several retaining walls as the valley narrows.

The road departs the Westfield for good here and finds its way between two sections of the Hiram Fox Wildlife Management Area, staying with the Little River, which abruptly comes into view on the right. At 20.4 miles, entering South Worthington, you cross the Little River. There is a deadwater along here on the right fed by Jackson Brook. The deadwater gives way to Eagle Ridge further along in Ringville. Passing a concert center, an old farmhouse, and a sugarhouse, you will see hill views begin to open up across a field. Go over the Little River next and look toward higher ridges to the east in the direction of Chesterfield. There are increasingly good views westward, too, after you ascend a long hill and pass Radiker Road on the right, where there are orchards, open fields, and signs of maple sugaring operations at 24.6 miles. By any measure, this is real country.

You roll next (at 26 miles) through old-fashioned Worthington, with its continuous "lawns" connecting a series of stately older homes and community buildings along the green. The place has the flavor of many an earlier New England settlement where people lived close together and remoteness hadn't much value. Just beyond, you approach Worthington Corners, pass the Worthington Health Care Center, and go by the

Worthington Inn. The Worthington Museum and Library, welcoming old wooden structures both, also stand here at the Corners.

Watch for the turn now as you leave MA 112 and *go left* on MA 143, heading northwest into more rural countryside where 143 climbs to the east of Fox Den Wildlife Management Area and West Hill. At 27.4 miles you'll have more outlooks over rolling hills to eastward. The wandering route loops gradually north and then southward into West Worthington, climbing steadily as it approaches the Peru line, at 30.8 miles. You then zigzag westward and uphill through a series of S-curves beneath dense hardwood canopy as you leave Hampshire County for Berkshire County.

The steady upward effort on this stretch should not come as a surprise. You're in the very heart of the Berkshire Range now and ascending a rise between French and Peru Hills, both of which are over 2,100 feet in elevation. The road adopts this high, wooded plateau, crosses over the line into Hinsdale at 36.2 miles, and crosses the narrows of pretty Ashmere Lake as you roll due west. A low, marshy area surrounded by swamp maples, which backs up to Cleveland Brook Reservoir well to the north, appears presently on your right.

Pass the fire station and come to the First Congregational Church in a mixed residential and business area of Hinsdale, *bearing right* at the junction of MA 143 and 8 at 38.8 miles. Follow MA 8 north and twice cross the East Branch of the Housatonic River near Old Dalton Road. With Tully and Day Mountains off to the left, you enter the attractive, quiet community of Dalton at 40 miles and follow the winding road north into the town center, passing by the regiional high school and ending this drive in front of the Crane Community Center after 43.1 miles of travel.

To see western Massachusetts's most interesting cultural centers, you can reach Lenox, Stockbridge, and Great Barrington from Dalton by traveling farther west on MA 9 and taking US 7 or 7A south through Pittsfield. Williamstown and North Adams, to the north, are reached via US 7 north or MA 8 and 2.

9

Route
Newburyport to Manchester-by-the-Sea
Highway
MA 1A, 133, Southern Avenue, School Street
Distance
23 miles

Here's a route that takes you through the best of the North Shore's inner cape country, dropping southward from the Bay State's northernmost coastal community to attractive Ipswich, through historic Essex, and on to patrician Manchester-by-the-Sea. Following US 1A, the drive avoids the more hurried traffic on US 1 and nearby I-95.

Newburyport, point of departure for this outing, has always been one of my favorite cities. It's a small place where the old and new mingle comfortably, a town with the look of belonging and not some paver's mad dream of asphalt and concrete. Several decades ago, certain geniuses wanted to tear down the town's old center and erect that ugly miasmatic concoction of prestressed concrete and neon that passes for community in a lot of today's America. Locals who couldn't see the benefit of such cleverness rose up, and a good deal of the remarkable old waterfront neighborhood was saved. Today it stands as a splendid red-brick tribute to the beauty and fittingness of what came before. Present day Newbury-

 Home to Essex history

port has an interesting, welcoming downtown with real shops and restaurants and little evidence of the hideous chain-store malaise so common everywhere. (Those have been kept at bay out near I-95.)

Newburyport lies at the mouth of New England's great Merrimack River, a waterway that has its estimable beginnings well northward in central New Hampshire, and which forms an acquaintance with many a northeast city and town before emptying into the Atlantic here. Newburyport also boasts a superb harbor, protected as it is by an extensive barrier beach in the form of Plum Island. It was from this harbor that patriot Benedict Arnold launched his waterborne campaign against British Quebec in 1775. Arnold's fleet, cobbled together of working craft from Newburyport waters, sailed past Plum Island Point and north to Maine's Kennebec River, which reaches northwestward toward Quebec.

Both the Merrimack and the Parker Rivers feed Plum Island Sound,

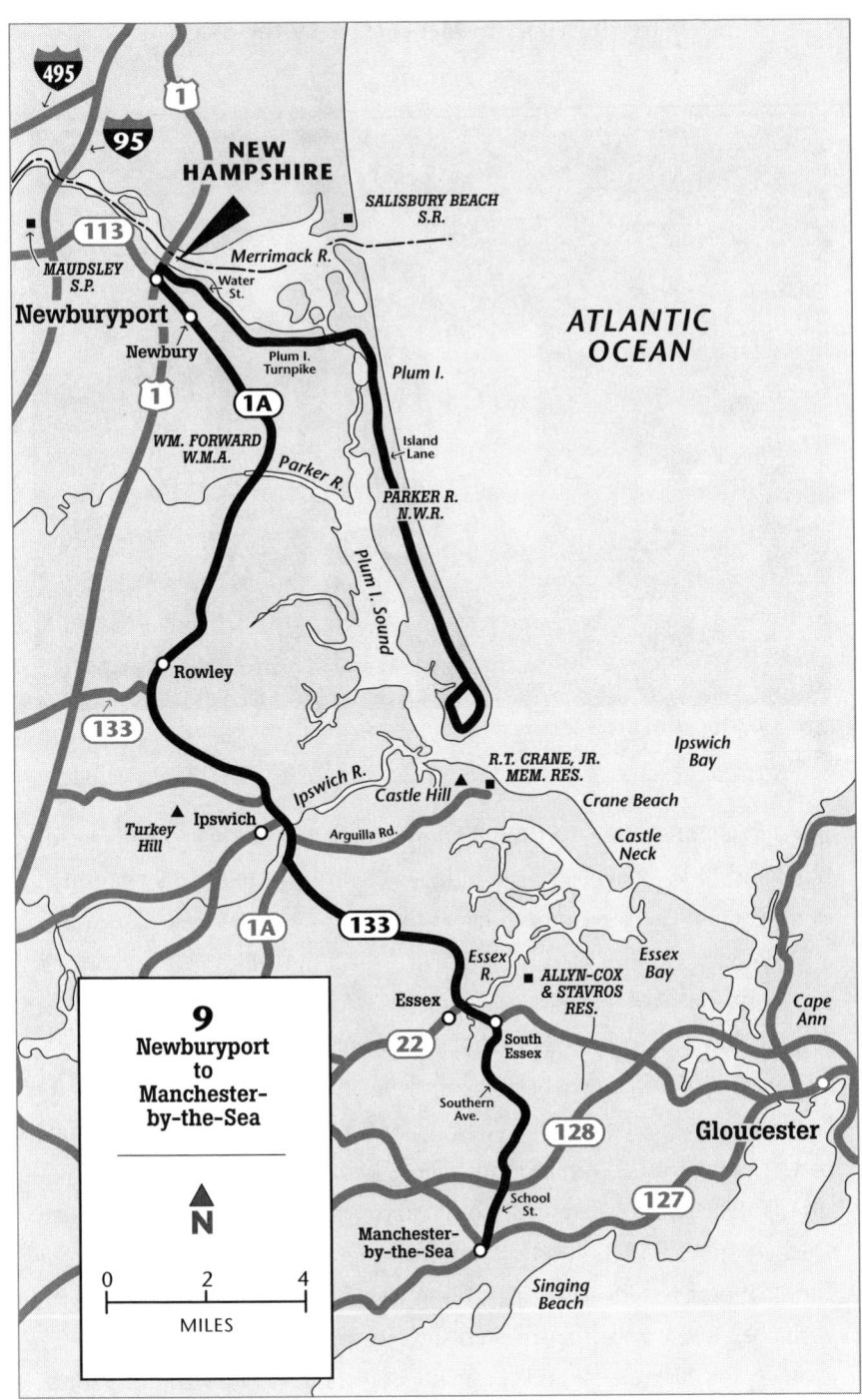

which in turn lubricates the extensive marshes that lie behind Plum Island and to landward at adjacent Newbury. Plum Island is itself a local treasure. Its northern tip is despoiled by a cottage jumble, but the rest of the island is wonderfully preserved as the Parker River National Wildlife Refuge. One can walk on Plum for hours along marsh, woodland, dunes, and spectacular beach. This spit of land is a birders' paradise, with all manner of migrating species using it as a stopping-off place. Wandering the marshes, I have come within touching distance of somnolent great horned owls and have regularly seen resident northern harriers and such interesting seasonal visitors as snowy owls and purple martins. Occasionally, rare northern seabirds are spotted here, too—with flocks of birders armed with impressive telescopes fast on their trail, adding to life lists.

Before heading south, visit the island by taking Water Street downtown. Water Street soon becomes the Plum Island Turnpike, leading to the National Wildlife Refuge. Massachusetts Audubon operates an important birding center along this route. You enter the Plum Island reservation to the right once over the bridge. Starting out as a 1,600-acre Audubon preserve, which was joined to 3,000-plus acres of federal lands in 1941, the Parker River National Wildlife Refuge on Plum Island now encompasses more than 4,600 acres.

Also nearby, on Newburyport's west side, Maudslay State Park welcomes walkers, and Salisbury Beach State Reservation, across the Merrimack river, beckons beach strollers and swimmers. An informal walk around Newburyport has its rewards, too; the place is chock full of great old Federal-style buildings, especially along High Street (MA 133 and US 1A). Two of these interesting domiciles, the grand Cushing House and the simpler 1654 Coffin House, plus the Customhouse Maritime Museum on Water Street, are must-visits (open seasonally).

From the junction of State Street and US 1A in central Newburyport, begin this saunter by *going southeast* on 1A, almost immediately crossing into Newbury and passing the Coffin House as you go. The road continues southeast here behind the great marshes bisected by Pine Island Creek, and then turns more southward to the Parker River. Off to the right, along Newman Road, lies Old Town Hill—worth a short climb to its low summit for elevated views seaward. (See the author's *Weekend Walks on the New England Coast* for hikes in this area.) The woodlands of the William Forward Wildlife Management Area are to the right upriver as you cross the Parker's broad channel. The river extends back westward for miles, flushing an enormous area of wild marshland all the way to Byfield. The salt marshes here show evidence of the old practice of taking in salt hay: remnants of hay stook platforms from another era can be seen in the marsh. The hay was carried in horse-drawn wagons or by scow westward to drier ground dotted with saltwater farms.

Beyond the river, you cross into Rowley in another 3 miles, approaching the Forward Wildlife Management Area to the right as 1A works its way farther to the southwest. To the left here are fine views of the great seaward marshes cut by the Rowley River. Holy and Rogers Islands stand far off at the river's mouth. Minutes later, you pass through the pleasant, sedate little center of Rowley, replete with attractive white-fronted Victorian and Federal houses. You come then to a junction where MA 133 joins 1A less than a mile south of Rowley center. The two now run together as the road pulls sharply to the southeast and passes two small ponds on the left at a meeting of Bull Brook and the Egypt River. With Turkey Hill to the right, you now enter a more built-up area, cross the rail line, and come into Ipswich center and the shopping district. Ipswich shows its age in a pleasant, comfortable way. The quiet, leafy village contains many older houses that are relics of the earliest days of settlement.

Route 1A pulls *right and south* at the five points intersection in Ipswich and steps over the Ipswich River, then runs south along a green backed by fine old saltboxes. For an interesting side trip, Argilla Road leaves left, finding its way through the marshes to the Richard Crane Jr.

 At the green, Old Ipswich

Memorial Reservation, otherwise known simply as Castle Hill. An adjacent and highly popular beach occupies Crane Neck and leans southeast from the coastal drumlin on which Crane's great mansion is situated. Once a monastic center, Castle Hill has in recent years become a sometime concert venue. Administered by the Trustees of Reservations, both the Great House and the beach are open to visitors in season for the price of admission.

Once back on the main route, *stay left* with MA 133 when it pulls away from 1A and run southeast through open, rolling farm country and scattered woodlands, crossing the Castle Neck River and entering Essex. Skirting the extensive marshlands of Essex Bay to the left, 133 turns southward to its junction with MA 22 in Essex by the Essex River, in a creekside neighborhood full of boat moorings, strangely fragrant clam shacks, and interesting local shops. Here, the Essex Shipbuilding Museum confirms the region's early importance as a center of skilled nauti-

In the village of Manchester-by-the-Sea

cal craftsmanship. Schooners in the Gloucester trade, dogbodies, pinkies, and all manner of coastal work boats were built here in more than two dozen shipyards perched along the river in the late 1800s. The Allyn-Cox and Stavros Reservations are two local preserves worth exploration, if secluded riverine back marsh suits your fancy. At its headquarters at the Allyn-Cox Reservation off MA 133, the Essex County Greenbelt Association offers a guide to hiking the various lands it protects.

Newburyport to Manchester-by-the-Sea

From the east side of Essex, leave MA 133 now and *go right* on Southern Avenue toward Manchester. You pull away from the shoreline here and go south and southeast through a rural. residential neighborhood. Three miles from Essex center, cross the town line of Manchester-by-the-Sea. Here you go over Sawmill Brook and cross MA 128, shortly coming into the village of Manchester on what is now School Street. Arrive at the conclusion of this drive at an intersection with MA 127 near pretty Manchester Harbor.

This community, once home to great resort hotels and droves of summerites, is now very much an upscale residential community with historic roots going back to its days in the Caribbean trade. The Manchester Historical Society houses its interesting collections in the old Trask House on Union Street. The town's ancestors reside in Summer Street's serene Old Burial Ground. Right downtown, on Central Street, you'll find the traditional tall spire of the Orthodox Congregational Church, a kind of beacon at the town's center. Summer days bring seasonal concerts at Masconomo Park on Beach Street. If you can't bear to be this close to the ocean without being *in* it, stroll out to Singing Beach, where nonlocals are admitted (though parking and beach house use are restricted to Manchester residents).

One could, by the way, do this drive in reverse with equally salutary results. Cruising this tidewater region and arriving in either Manchester or Newburyport at dusk on a warm summer evening is bound to be agreeable whether you follow this route traveling south or north. ⚓

10

Route

Nahant, Lynn, Swampscott,
Marblehead, Salem

Highway

Nahant Road, the Lynnway,
Lynn Shore Drive, MA 1A, 114

Distance

17 miles

Located far from the Bay State's rural farm and hill country, this short, interesting drive is, in its way, avowedly urban. The attraction here is of a different sort: a wander through old, established oceanfront neighborhoods, some so much at sea as to be connected to the mainland by only the narrowest of threads, others historic and utterly colonial-era in flavor. These communities at the lip of Boston's North Shore form a kind of transition outward toward Cape Ann, beginning outside the densely commercial and industrial zone that spreads north and east from Boston through East Boston, Chelsea, Winthrop, Revere, and Lynn. This drive from the shores of Lynn Harbor and Nahant Bay, north through Swampscott to old Marblehead, and then farther north to historic Salem, explores the periphery of Massachusetts Bay and the smaller harbors above it, arriving eventually in the midst of the intriguing witches' city.

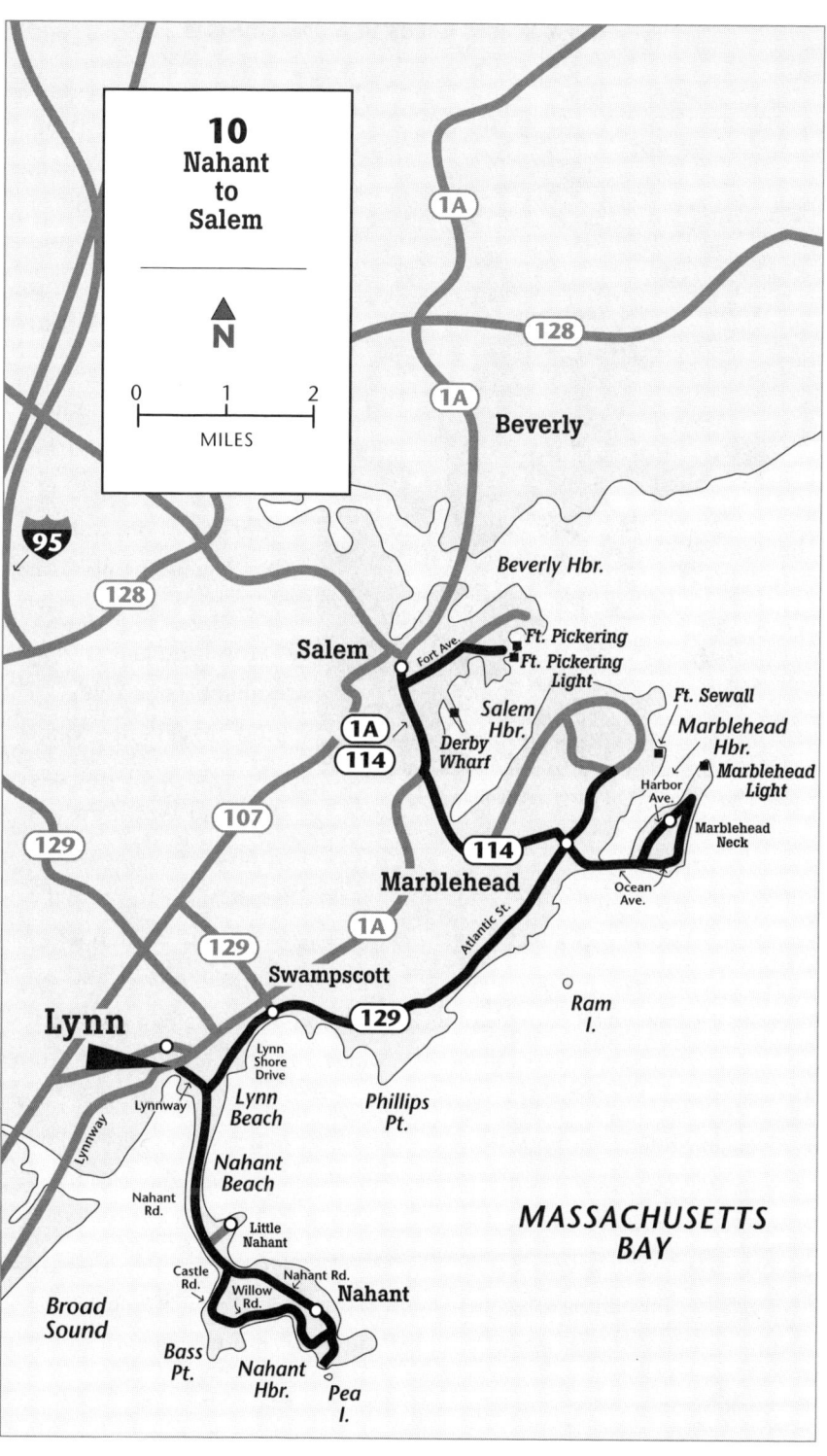

10
Nahant
to
Salem

▲
N

0   1   2
MILES

95

128

129

Lynn

128

1A

1A

Beverly

Beverly Hbr.

Salem

Ft. Pickering
Ft. Pickering
Light

1A
114

Fort Ave.

Salem
Hbr.

Derby
Wharf

Ft. Sewall

Marblehead
Hbr.

Marblehead
Light

Harbor
Ave.

Marblehead
Neck

114

Marblehead

Ocean
Ave.

107

129

1A

Swampscott

129

Atlantic St.

Ram
I.

Lynn
Shore
Drive

Lynnway

Lynn
Beach

Phillips
Pt.

Nahant Beach

**MASSACHUSETTS
BAY**

Nahant
Rd.

Little
Nahant

Castle
Rd.

Willow
Rd.

Nahant Rd.

Nahant

Nahant Rd.

**Broad
Sound**

Bass
Pt.

Nahant
Hbr.

Pea
I.

A ghost of early settlement, historic Salem

Begin this trip in Lynn at the busy intersection of the Lynnway and Nahant Road beside Lynn Beach and the Nahant Beach and Lynn Shore Reservation. Leaving the industrial zone along the Lynnway behind you, *head south* on Nahant Road, which follows a narrow isthmus between Lynn Harbor and Nahant Bay. You will find excellent water views here in the direction of Winthrop and Boston—where a constant stream of jet aircraft ascends from Logan International Airport in the southwest—and other views over Nahant Bay to the left. A number of parking areas here along Nahant Beach provide stopping places and access to the waterside. Crowds of locals and Bostonians flock to the beach on warm summer days to swim and enjoy the cool breezes that drift across this narrow neck of land.

Nahant Road shortly passes a compact little settlement to leftward on a nub of land known as Little Nahant. Just beyond it, roughly two miles along, *go right* in another residential neighborhood in Nahant proper on Castle Road. Follow Castle Road to an intersection with Willow Road in the neighborhood known as Bass Point. There are occasional water views here as you *go left and east* on Willow Road, next skirting Nahant Harbor.

In summer, this protected anchorage is mightily busy with local boating and sailing activity.

Follow Willow Street back to Nahant Road, *turning right and southeast* again and follow Nahant Road until you can't go any farther. The road ends at Great Ledge, the very tip of the isthmus, opposite Pea Island. There are oceanward views here: to the north, across Nahant Bay, lies Swampscott, and farther eastward is Marblehead; southward, one can see the numerous islands of Boston Harbor beyond Broad Sound; immediately southwestward is Winthrop, the major promontory tipped by Deer Island. Seasonal ferries to Salem and Gloucester cruise jauntily by during the summer.

Turn about when you're ready and head north on Nahant Road again, returning to your starting point at the Lynnway. *Go right* here and continue along the water's edge heading *north* along Lynn Beach on Lynn Shore Drive. This is sometimes a busy section of road, the seasonal congestion made more tolerable by dramatic seaward outlooks to the right. Lynn Shore Drive becomes Humphrey Street as you enter Swampscott, its waterfront marked by attractive, large homes and apartment buildings plus the occasional inn or bed-and-breakfast establishment. Swampscott was once home to a number of distinguished local boatbuilders, and this expanse of Atlantic waterfront hosted races and regattas for locally built craft. The redoubtable and ever handy Swampscott dory, rigged for sailing, owes its design to these local shops. The Swampscott is a lasting tribute to the ability of local craftsmen to adapt the rough, steep-sided Grand Banks dory to pleasure cruising, its new lines softened and rounded to be more efficient and more pleasing to the eye. The broad, open waters through which these workboat regattas and races moved are visible to the right as you travel north here.

Staying above the shore, you pull more to the northeast and join MA 129 (east), brushing by Phillips Point and then Phillips Beach. You next cross into Marblehead, opposite Ram Island. MA 129, known here as Atlantic Street, rolls through rows of waterfront homes and arrives at a junction with Ocean Avenue in another mile and a half. A side trip out Ocean Avenue to the right brings one to attractive Devereux Beach, which lies along the causeway opposite Marblehead Harbor. Beyond it one finds the mansions and yacht clubs of Marblehead Neck, pretty Chandler Hovey Park, and Lighthouse Point. Marblehead Harbor is a deservedly favorite yachting destination in season, and whole fleets of sailing craft from clubs to the south drop anchor here as they progress along the New England coast. The sheltered harbor contains a veritable traffic jam of high-end sailing pretties in July and August.

Stay with MA 129 right into the business district of Marblehead and come to a junction with MA 114, watching for Washington Street on your right. *Turn right* here and roll uphill past doughty, steepled Abbott Hall and down toward the waterfront in the old town. Around Market Square, dominated by the brick, mortar, and clapboard island that is the lovely Old Town House, you'll find a fascinating tangle of streets with attractive period homes and shops cheek by jowl as they were built from the mid-1600s onward.

Those of us who are driving would do well to find a parking space anywhere in this neighborhood (a daunting task in high summer) and walk about the old district, where a collection of interesting shops, restaurants, and galleries beckons attention. Then a pleasant walk down State Street will take you to the waterfront and out to Fort Sewall. This eighteenth-century fortification at the mouth of the harbor provides outstanding views of the entrance to the sheltered waters opposite Marblehead Light.

Marblehead, as its architecture suggests, boasts colonial-era origins. As early as 1629 Mamaracia—or Marble Harbor, as it was sometimes named—saw the arrival of Channel Islanders and Cornishmen who established a community here as an offshoot of Puritan Salem. *Boston Globe* columnist Herbert Kenny quotes a local as saying, "Our ancestors came not here for religion. Their main end was to catch fish." No fear — the early community was certainly no tabernacle. Marblehead arose as a hodgepodge colony of fishing shacks and hovels, home of suspected witches, and notably a place of frequent misbehavior. When the Salem witch hysteria commenced, one of those enthusiastically hanged was Mammy Red, from

Old Salem

Marblehead, who, according to Kenny, showed a propensity for turning the butter of those she disliked into blue wool. A later era of prosperity brought the substantial houses that now characterize the old town, and Marblehead became its own self formally in 1829. Marblehead men crewed the USS *Constitution*, and the town, under the aegis of patriot John Glover, commissioned the *Hannah*, one of the first ships of war in the new colonies. The town wears its history comfortably today.

Retreating to the junction of MA 129 and MA 114, *take the latter northwest* toward Salem. The route skirts the southern tip of Salem Harbor, passes Salem State College, and wends its way through densely settled South Salem, where 114 joins MA 1A. Side streets to the right here

Salem's native son

lead to Salem 1630, a pioneer village restoration. Running together, 1A and 114 bring you to downtown Salem, where you should seek out East India Square and the Peabody Essex Museum. Park anywhere in the vicinity of the museum. The neighborhood is simply crammed with important historical sights, and they are best reached on foot.

The Peabody Essex Museum, a grand eighteenth-century amalgam of mostly Samuel McIntyre–inspired Federal architecture, consists of more than a dozen edifices holding maritime-oriented collections of the fine and decorative arts. Named for philanthropist George Peabody, the museum features holdings that reflect a community historically tied to ocean-borne commerce worldwide. The hub of the museum's structures is at Liberty Street and Essex Street off East India Square.

A short distance away, at Derby Wharf, are the Salem Maritime National Historic Site, the old Customs House, and the berthed sailing replica *Friendship*. The Salem Visitor Center, where New Liberty and Essex Streets meet, offers guides to local walks and other information about this interesting area of early houses and other buildings, including the nearby House of Seven Gables on Turner Street and the Salem Witch Museum on Washington Square.

Begun as the tiny settlement of Naumkeag after 1623, Salem had become by the late 1700s one of the most wealthy, active, and successful trading ports in the New World. The president of Yale University, Dr. Timothy Dwight, who toured the area before 1800, cheerfully pronounced Salem the sixth most commercially active town on the coast, sixth in population, and by all measures the most wealthy of any. Salem distinguished itself early on as a pioneer in the China trade, but was ultimately destined to lie in the shadow of Boston because its less than perfect harbor was intolerant of all but shallow-draft vessels. Yale's Dr. Dwight noted that, for fear of going aground, any vessel with a draft of more than twelve feet had to be unloaded by lighters well out from Salem's docks.

Salem was the home, real and thematic, of American author Nathaniel Hawthorne, who labored at the waterfront in a Customs House sinecure. His statue is mounted near the Essex Institute. The Salem of Hawthorne's ancestors served up enduring distress—and eventual death—to some of its inhabitants by virtue of an enthusiasm for hanging witches. Hawthorne gave life, in fictional form, to the mysterious *House of Seven Gables* and delivered up this period of darkness for universal consumption. The real witch hysteria took fire in the Danvers section of town in 1692, neighbor denouncing neighbor, and by the time the hardy Puritans had finished, fourteen women and five men had been hanged for satanic possession and a sixth man had been pressed to death. Another 150 unfortunates were jailed and interrogated but later released as the madness died down.

When you've thoroughly explored the historic zone, get back behind the wheel one last time and press on to nearby Fort Pickering by heading northeast out Salem Neck on Derby Street and Fort Avenue. The fort and lighthouse lie to the right about a mile from Derby Wharf. Named for Colonel Timothy Pickering, one-time quartermaster general of the Continental Army and secretary of state in the administrations of George Washington and John Adams, the fort guards the entrance to Salem Harbor. The Pickering family continues to have a presence in Salem, and the family manse, built in 1651, may be visited on Broad Street, where it is open to view on Mondays. Good harbor views across Beverly Harbor and out to Massachusetts Bay are yours here at Fort Pickering, where this drive ends. 🗝

11

Route
NORTH SHORE JOURNEY:
Bradford to Gloucester

Highway
Salem Street, MA 97, MA 133, Main Street,
MA 97, Cedar Street, Cherry Street, MA 1A, Larch Row,
Grapevine Road, Hart (Main) Street, MA 127

Distance
40 miles

For those who yearn to explore the back roads of the Bay State's North Shore, this route provides a grand diversion. Beginning in the river city of Haverhill, this trip meanders through the quiet rural towns of Bradford, Groveland, Georgetown, the Boxfords, and then on to the hunt-club neighborhoods of Hamilton and Wenham. From there, you'll head east through coastal Manchester by-the-Sea to the tip of salty Cape Ann. At the end of this drive you'll find proud Gloucester, still home of a large, active fishing fleet, its life oriented toward the riches of the fabled North Atlantic fishing banks.

Cape Ann, some would argue, was the Bay State's first oceanside playground. Massachusetts's lengthy North Shore, a chain of waterside towns and back villages, has been sometimes viewed as a superior place to visit

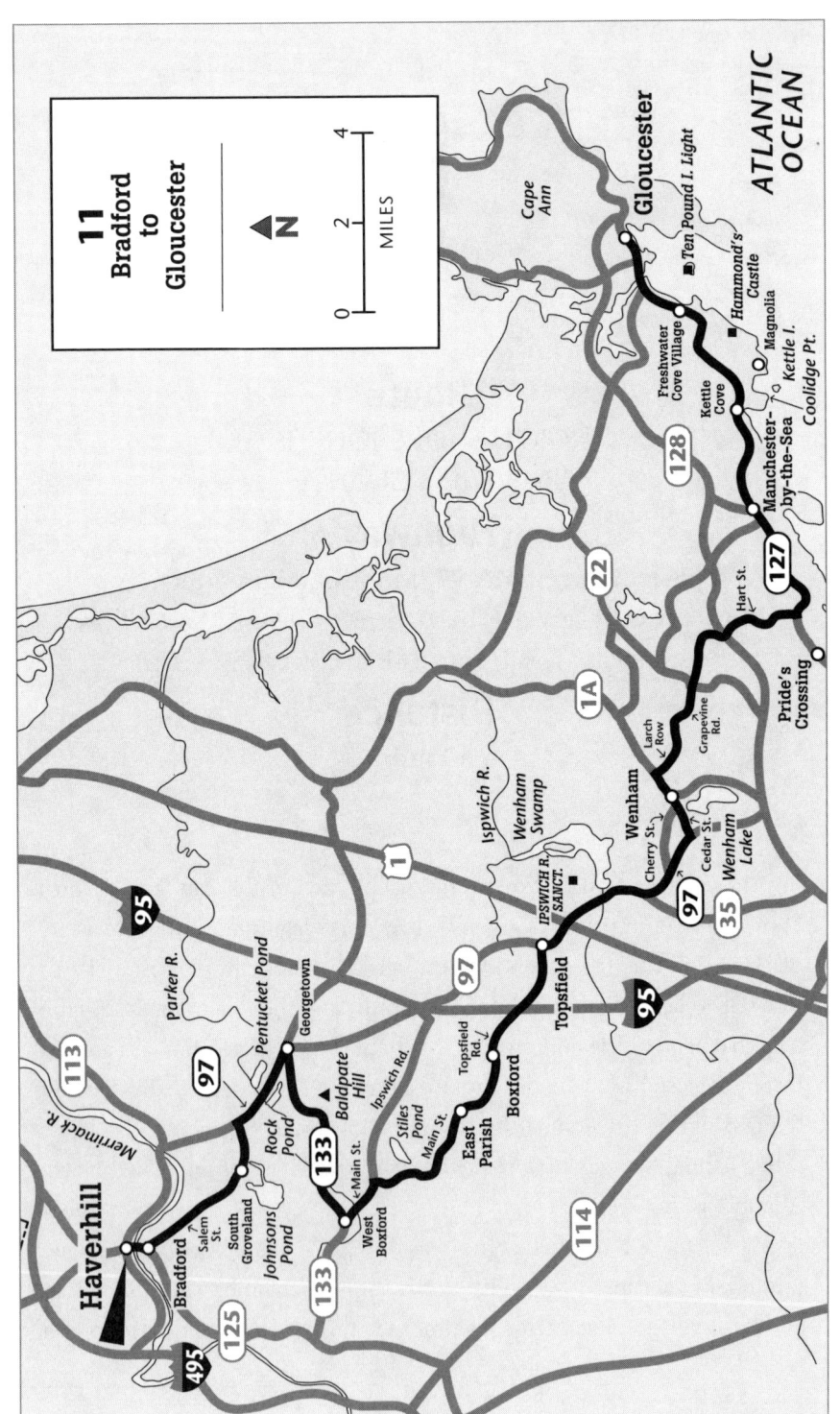

11
Bradford
to
Gloucester

N

0   2   4
MILES

ATLANTIC OCEAN

Gloucester
Ten Pound I. Light
Hammond's Castle
Freshwater Cove Village
Kettle Cove
Magnolia
Kettle I.
Coolidge Pt.
Manchester-by-the-Sea
128
127
Hart St.
Pride's Crossing
Larch Row
Grapevine Rd.
22
1A
Wenham
Cherry St.
Cedar St.
Wenham Lake
97
35
Ispwich R.
Wenham Swamp
1
IPSWICH R. SANCT.
Cape Ann
97
Topsfield
95
Topsfield Rd.
Boxford
East Parish
Main St.
Stiles Pond
Ipswich Rd.
West Boxford
Baldpate Hill
133
Main St.
133
95
Parker R.
Pentucket Pond
Georgetown
97
Rock Pond
114
113
Merrimack R.
Haverhill
Bradford
Salem St.
South Groveland
Johnsons Pond
125
495

or settle, a region very different from its noisier, congested sister cape to the southeast. Longtime *Boston Globe* editor and columnist Herb Kenny once noted how Cape Anners dismissed Cape Cod as a place of "long lines of flatulent automobiles like so many elephants locked tail to snout . . . flanked by neon signs flashing vulgar messages for intolerable road-side stands or garish motels with nauseatingly coy names...." North Shore defenders have always seen their own turf as quieter, more truly rural, and proudly tied to a historic past. Anyone driving this route will get a firsthand chance to join the discussion.

Begin this outing in the civilized inland precincts of downtown Haverhill by the broad banks of the winding Merrimack River. Take MA 125 *south* across the river to Bradford, and, at a common, *go left and southeast* on Salem Street, pulling away from MA 125. The road coasts out of town slowly, passing through neighborhoods of large older homes and by the Bradford Country Club. At just over a mile you are in more rural country, farm stands dotting the road as you go southeast. Pretty, rolling hills stand off to the north and left. You cross into Groveland shortly, at 2 miles, in woods and marshlands backed by a low rise to the south. Continue east, passing a flooded river trending to marsh on the right at 2.8 miles—a beautiful, wild-looking place. At 4.1 miles you reach a junction with MA 97, where you *turn right* and head for Georgetown on a broader parkway.

After going through a commercial area and under a power line, cross the Georgetown line at 4.6 miles and roll through rural residential countryside again, next crossing a swampy brook that connects hidden Pentucket Pond and Rock Pond, flanking the road, at 4.8 miles. The latter pond is fed via the lengthy Parker River drainage from the west. Pass 4-H Camp Lesley at 5.3 miles and come to the center of thriving Georgetown, where you *bear right and southwest* on MA 133, passing the town hall and the First Congregational Church, founded in 1732. The road gains elevation gradually here, and views off to the north begin to emerge

In the precincts of Cape Ann

as you pass Andover Hill Farm and scurry around Baldpate Hill to the left.

The route gets more densely wooded as you drift southwest past the Georgetown VFW. You now begin to follow the Parker River drainage closely on the right, cross the river, and have views of the extensive marsh on both left and right. Pass by a cluster of houses at 9.4 miles, with old stone walls to the right, and go by an intersection with Washington Street. Continue southwest to West Boxford, where you slow for a sharp *left* onto Main Street at 10.1 miles. Pass the American Legion Post and the village store on Main Street, and continue southward into rural countryside again at 10.7 miles. You will have occasional hilly views to the right over more stone walls and pasture, skirting a dormant pond at 10.9 miles.

Keep right at a junction on Main Street and then pass Stiles Pond Road at 12.3 miles in sparsely settled, wooded country. The few houses here are hidden and set back from the road. There are bogs to left and right now, a part of the dense Fish Brook deadwater, as the road swings through a hundred-acre lowland fed by Fish Brook. Pass an old farm at

13.1 miles and continue through heavily wooded country, which yields to fields periodically. There's a real feeling of remoteness here. You go by another farm at 14.3 miles and then cruise south-southeast beside a line of pretty stone walls at just under 15 miles. Here you ride through junctions with Lawrence and Towne Roads in a neighborhood known as East Parish. After coming into an area of fine older houses, you pull to the north briefly on Main Street and then *keep right* at the Boxford village green, next going *east* on Topsfield Road under a canopy of giant maples.

Drifting southeast in a thickly wooded residential neighborhood, Topsfield Road goes over I-95 at 17 miles. The road navigates through a column of cedars and then crosses the Topsfield town line at 17.9 miles. Continue into Topsfield center on what is now Washington Street. At the Topsfield common you'll watch for MA 97 at 18.5 miles, where you *bear right and southeast* by the Congregational Church. Following MA 97 toward Wenham, you next cross US 1 and leap over the Ipswich River, where there are pretty views to the left and right. Leftward, the river backs up to the east and north, creating the vast Wenham Swamp. Nearby is the 2,800-acre Ipswich River Wildlife Sanctuary, with facilities operated by Massachusetts Audubon. There are excellent hiking and cross-country ski trails here in extensive protected marsh and woodlands (see the author's *Weekend Walks on the New England Coast* for details).

MA 97 bends to the southwest, passes MA 35 on the right at 21.6 miles, and then goes southeast again, crossing the Wenham line in wild, partially flooded marshland studded with moldering hardwood trunks. Some nice views leftward follow at 22.1 miles before you run into a more built-up area and, at 23.4 miles, *go left and northeast* on Cedar Street to Wenham center. In minutes you'll pass the wooded shore of very beautiful Wenham Lake to the south and right.

Prepare to do some careful navigating now. *Keep right* on Cherry Street at 25.1 miles and follow it to a junction with MA 1A, where you *go left and northeast*. Drive a few blocks past the common, the Wenham

Museum, and the First Church in Wenham, watching closely for Larch Row on the right. *Bear right and south* on Larch Row at just under 26 miles and proceed south, then east, through what only can be described as one of the Bay State's most sumptuous, "old money" residential areas. Go through some open fields and cross a rail line, soon passing the rolling fields of the Cabot Farm at 26.7 miles, and then bearing right and south on Grapevine Road at 27.5 miles, toward Beverly Farms. Grapevine Road meets MA 22, skirts a chain of lakes to its left, and passes through a rural residential area, soon arriving at the campus of Gordon College. Passing the college at 29.8 miles, cross over MA 128 and continue south on what is now variously known as Hart Street or Main Street.

At 30.2 miles, pass the Massachusetts Audubon Society's Endicott Reservation, round a marsh and cross the Beverly town line, continuing south to Beverly Farms. You pass the architecturally interesting North Shore Community Baptist Church as you navigate around the north side of the built-up zone and work past town. You begin to have limited ocean views off to the south here as you *turn left and northeast* shortly on MA 127 at 32.1 miles. Following 127, you go by the Brookwood and the Landmark Schools, crossing the Manchester-by-the-Sea line at 32.8 miles. There are excellent harbor views to the right as you come into the center of Manchester at 33.9 miles and proceed through its appealing, narrow streets past the green.

In 1629, Manchester, then known as Jeffries Creek, saw the landing of the British ship *Talbot*, whose chaplain referred fulsomely to the "fyne and sweet harbour, seven miles from the head of Cape Ann." Manchester became a fishing and trading community and later a place of furniture craftsmanship, perhaps initially a good deal less elegant than its modern-day inhabitants would have preferred, but its permanence as a community was assured.

At the rail station, *continue eastward* at just over 34 miles, *staying with MA 127* as it then heads on toward Gloucester. Pass a ball field and pull

Gloucester sentinel

into less densely built-up countryside, still heading northeast on 127, going under a rail line. Horses in fields give this area a rural feeling. Beyond the pastures, you lean southeast, passing occasional water views and going through Kettle Cove village at 35.3 miles, opposite Kettle Island. Then the road heads east-northeast again, missing Magnolia proper, and passes the seaside Coolidge Reservation and Coolidge Point at 36.2 miles. This preserve, administered by Massachusetts's unique Trustees of Reservations, is open to the public. Visiting hours are posted.

The grand architecture of Magnolia's secluded baronial homes gives way to the everyday world as you cross the Gloucester town line at 36.6 miles. With hills to the right and swampy ground to the left, you pass connectors to fabled Hammond's Castle, former home of prodigious master inventor John Hays Hammond. The road winds and turns northeastward here, passing more preservation lands at 38.1 miles. MA 127 next goes through Freshwater Cove Village, where at 39 miles there are pleasing water views both on right and left.

Pulling first north and then east, MA 127 brings you now to Gloucester Harbor as it crosses a channel and arrives at Stage Fort Park, where early fishermen began planting their nets to oceanward as early as 1623. The Gloucester Welcoming Center is here, too, a valuable information source (open seasonally). Leonard Craske's famous Gloucester Fisherman's Monument lies just beyond, across the Blynman Bridge on Stacy Boulevard. The drive ends now as splendid harbor vistas span the southern horizon. The prominent feature is Ten Pound Light, which is in turn backed by distinctive Eastern Point. Find a place to leave the car, and immerse yourself in the interesting and attractive downtown area of Gloucester, a small city of immense legend always worthy of a visitor's attention. ⚓

12

Route
Gloucester–Rockport
Outer Cape Ann Loop
Highway
MA 127A, 127
Distance
18 miles

This shorter but quite engaging drive around the tip of Cape Ann collects water views, tangy seaside enclaves, beaches, and lighthouses. Beginning and ending in Gloucester, the route wanders through Annisquam and Rockport, traveling at water level by striking Annisquam Harbor, capturing Annisquam Light, and pausing at Bearskin Neck and "Motif Number One." The route then returns to the west of Straitsmouth Island Light, Thacher Island Twin Lights, and Gloucester's exclusive Eastern Point peninsula near Ten Pound Light. This drive begs you, time and again, to pause along your way and explore on foot, perhaps with binoculars and camera in hand, some of the great sights of ocean-bounded outermost Cape Ann. By the time you've completed this very leisurely eighteen-mile loop, you'll be spoiled for inland living forever.

Whether you preface this drive with an exploration of Gloucester's downtown or make the rounds on your return, the fabled coastal city

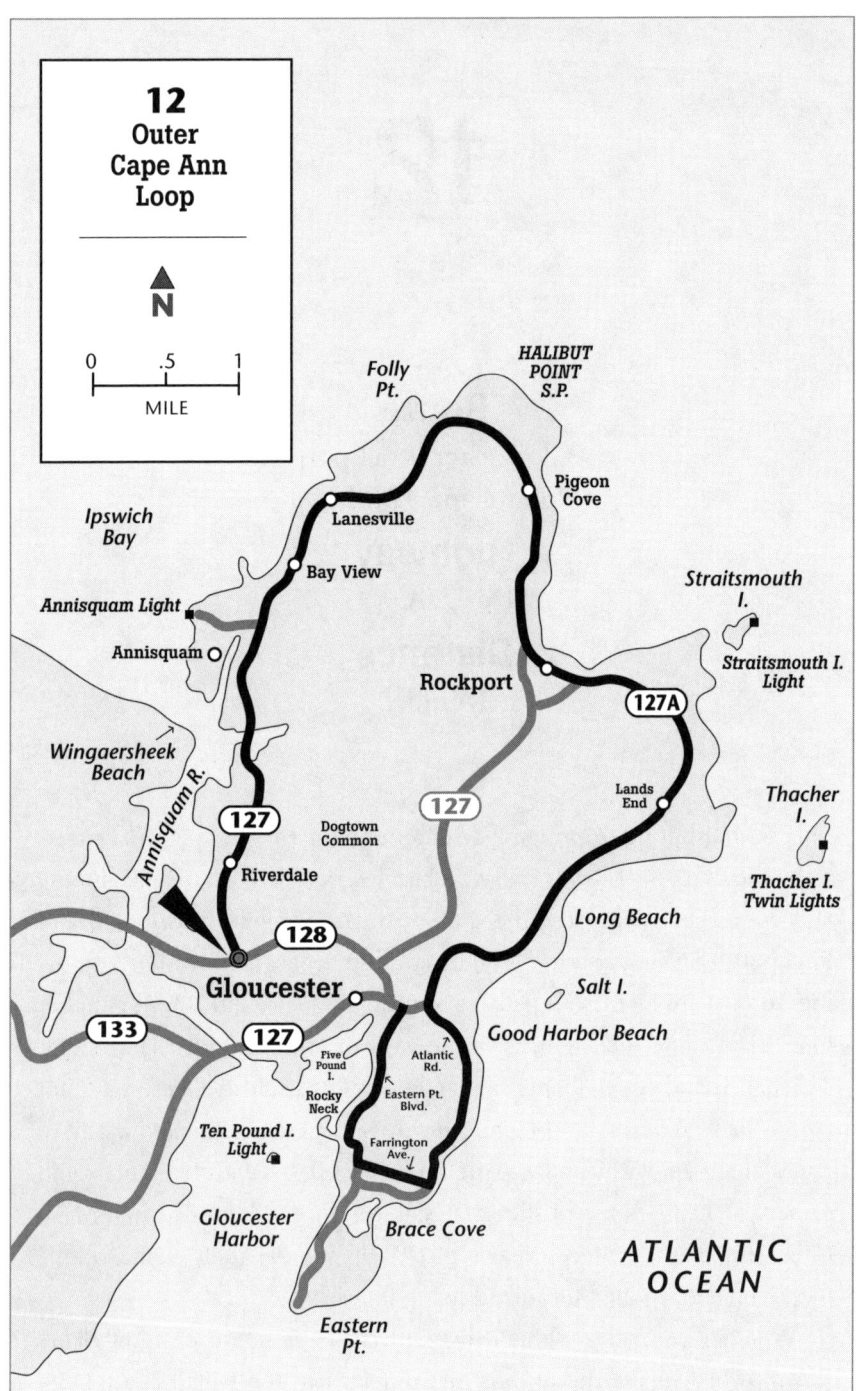

12
Outer Cape Ann Loop

N

0   .5   1
MILE

Folly Pt.

HALIBUT POINT S.P.

Lanesville

Pigeon Cove

Ipswich Bay

Bay View

Straitsmouth I.

Annisquam Light

Annisquam

Straitsmouth I. Light

Rockport

127A

Wingaersheek Beach

Thacher I.

Lands End

127

Dogtown Common

127

Thacher I. Twin Lights

127

Riverdale

128

Long Beach

Gloucester

Salt I.

133

127

Good Harbor Beach

Five Pound I.

Atlantic Rd.

Rocky Neck

Eastern Pt. Blvd.

Ten Pound I. Light

Farrington Ave.

Gloucester Harbor

Brace Cove

ATLANTIC OCEAN

Eastern Pt.

welcomes investigating. Gloucester, like New Bedford, boasts a proud Portuguese lineage embedded in an old Yankee frame. Shops, bakeries, and restaurants sometimes show evidence of this Portuguese heritage, but in a practical way: Gloucester is not a "chi-chi" seaside habitation, as so much of the shoreline has become, but a real, working city where people are rightfully proud of their way of life. The Cape Ann Museum on Pleasant Street will introduce you to that history and to the regional art that has sprung from it. A self-guided walking tour of the city along the Maritime Trail is interesting; ask for the brochure in local shops and eateries. For walkers, 500-acre Ravenswood Park off MA 127 in West Gloucester offers miles of hiking trails as well.

Take to the road at Gloucester's west side rotary, where MA 128 and 127 intersect just east of the bridge spanning the rangy Annisquam River. *Take 127 north* toward Annisquam. The road drifts through a built-up residential area that backs up to fabled Dogtown Common, an abandoned community in the woods to the east of here that was rumored to be home to a whole colony of misfits, sea types, hooligans, and the disaffected. Dogtown began as a seventeenth-century fishing settlement, and during the Depression it became a notable "Hooverville," a stopping place for many without jobs or connections. It is possible, as I've done on a number of occasions, to walk from here all the way to Rockport center through the brush and hardwoods that obscure the site of that interesting but now vanished community. You can't see the Dogtown trail from MA 127, but will be able to find it if you take one of the residential side streets to the right of the highway. The trail departs from a gravel pit behind the houses.

MA 127 north heads through the River Landing and Riverdale sections of Gloucester. The road curves around Ipswich Bay and crosses its inlet, with attractive water views north and south. You then pull north again at 1.2 miles, passing a school and proceeding to the Annisquam portion of Gloucester. The road drops to water level shortly and passes

 At Halibut Point, Cape Ann

the point where the Annisquam River widens to become Annisquam Harbor, with outlooks westward to Wingaersheek Beach in West Gloucester at 2.3 miles. The road travels northeast along the north cove of the harbor, a very pretty anchorage, and climbs past a footbridge. You come to a junction by a church at 3.1 miles, *keeping right and northeast* on 127 toward Bay View and Lanesville. Watch for a side street to the left shortly, which will take you out to Annisquam Light by Wigwam Point. The light overlooks Ipswich Bay, with fine views northwest to Castle Neck and Newburyport's Plum Island.

MA 127 narrows as it winds into Bay View, a place, not surprisingly, gifted with more good views northwestward over Ipswich Bay. There is also a University of Massachusetts marine biology research station here. The road then continues northward through a series of attractive residential neighborhoods and, at 4.2 miles, rounds the bend in Lanesville

Early hours at Gloucester

by Sacred Heart Church, then passes the tiny Lanesville post office at 4.5 miles. The drift is now east and northeast to a junction with Washington Street at 5.4 miles, where next you pass a side road on your left to Folly Cove Landing. Just beyond, cross into Rockport at 5.7 miles, where to the left shortly there are fine open ocean views and signs for Halibut Point. The point is the northernmost outcrop of this large island that is Gloucester and Rockport. You'll find a small state park here with more excellent water exposures, which some argue afford views all the way to the New Hampshire and southern Maine coast in fair weather. Don't miss it.

Rockport broke away from Gloucester and became an independent community in 1840, having previously been known since 1753 simply as the Cape Parish of Gloucester. Marbleheader Richard Tarr and his family seem to have been the first settlers here, arriving around 1690 in what was then referred to as Sandy Bay. The fine-grained granite that underlies

Rockport, on Cape Ann

this bit of the New England coast became the area's economic mainstay, and the product of local quarries was sent down the coast to great cities for building.

You turn south now—traversing other close little neighborhoods wrapped around narrow, winding streets—and pass Pigeon Cove at 7 miles, coming next to some buildings remaining from Rockport's granite quarrying days. MA 127 is aptly named Granite Street here. You pass Pigeon Cove Chapel at 7.2 miles and round Sandy Bay southward, with spectacular views of the Atlantic to your left and of Rockport center to the southeast. Follow 127 into the village and, opposite the Sandy Bay Historical Society Museum at 8.5 miles, *make a left* onto King Street by the granite Rockport National Bank building.

At Beach Street, *go right* along the waterfront past Rockport's tiny pocket beach at the northwest end of the shopping area and restaurant district. In seconds, just past the Old Parish Burying Ground, *go right* and uphill on one-way Main Street to a wide intersection with MA 127 again. There *pull left* around to MA 127A, which will take you down to the heart of the commercial waterfront, where Rockport brims with shops, galleries, and eateries. Around back you'll find "Motif Number One," often said to be the most painted coastal scene in America. Walking up Main Street and out Rockport's colorful if over-touristy Bearskin Neck will keep you pleasantly occupied for a couple of hours if you choose to explore on foot. *Boston Globe* columnist Herb Kenny has surmised that the neck takes its name from an early escapade here in the late 1600s, when local Ebenezer Babson slew a bear with a hunting knife and skinned the animal on the spot. A barbecued-bear buffet apparently followed.

From here, it's off to East Gloucester via 127A as you roll uphill and eastward through a residential section. Several side streets to the left provide access to views of Straightsmouth Island Light to the northeast. Barely a mile from Rockport's waterfront, 127A leans to the south in the neighborhood known as Lands End. Make a loop through the side streets to the left again to views of the dramatic and unusual twin lighthouses of Thacher Island, less than a mile offshore. At 12.7 miles the road passes some marshland to the right in a section of cottages at Cape Hedge and, as it goes by Long Beach, crosses the Gloucester line at 13.2 miles. The road now leads westward and soon passes the entrance to beautiful Good Harbor Beach opposite Salt Island. Good Harbor is easily one of the finest stretches of coastal sand north of Boston. You continue west through a great expanse of marsh grass and soon come to a major crossroads in a shopping area where you leave 127 A, *going directly across* the intersection and south toward Eastern Point.

Follow Atlantic Road as it meanders through a section of expansive older homes on the bluffs, and then stay with the water's edge as Atlantic Road leads south, high above the open ocean. If you look well back over your left shoulder toward the northeast, you'll see the Thacher Island lights again. Just north of Brace Cove at 16.5 miles, *go right* on Farrington Avenue and cut west across the neck through some undeveloped wooded ground, shortly reaching views of more protected Gloucester

Harbor at 17 miles. Go by the gated entrance to Eastern Point—now off-limits to mere mortals such as us, though bus-tour types are willingly ushered in. *Keep right and north* now, working your way back toward the center of Gloucester along Eastern Point Boulevard.

A sandy beach offers open views to the left across the harbor to stubby Ten Pound Light, where artist Winslow Homer spent a summer capturing the harbor on canvas before taking himself northward to Prouts Neck in Maine. Some attractive harbor outlooks crop up from time to time as you slowly come back into town. You will pass the Rocky Neck art colony at 17.6 miles and go by the entrances to several marinas choked with sailing craft in season. Rocky Neck has long been the artists' corner of Gloucester. Childe Hassam, who would later become a habitué of the Isles of Shoals, worked here, as did John Sloan. Other painters followed, and they still do today. The route rounds Five Pound Island and shortly reaches 127A again, where this drive ends at just over 18 miles. From here, you can follow 127A west to its junction with MA 128 and MA 127 or take local roads to explore Gloucester center ✈.

13

Route
Carlisle to Wayland,
Great Meadows National Wildlife Refuge

Highway
MA 225, 62, Walden Street,
MA 126, South Great Road, Sudbury Road,
Concord Road, Lincoln Road,
Sherman Bridge Road, MA 126

Distance
22.3 miles

This north-south drive just west of Boston proves that a lot of attractive and interesting countryside is one's for the taking without driving too far from the Hub. The route clings to the Great Meadows National Wildlife Refuge (NWR), a gem of unspoiled wetland that shapes itself around the meandering Concord and Sudbury Rivers as they wend southward. It also offers several convenient places to get out of the car and make contact with the refuge and to relax in quiet countryside.

The journey begins in Carlisle at the junction of Lowell and Concord Streets with MA 225. *Travel 225 southeast* in the direction of Bedford and roll through a rural residential landscape, passing River Road and Skelton Road on the right at just over 2 miles. A little beyond, on both the

 Great Meadows National Wildlife Refuge

left and right, you reach the corridor of land that comprises the northern end of the Great Meadows NWR. Here the road crosses the Concord River, about which Henry David Thoreau wrote so revealingly in the mid-1800s. *A Week on the Concord and Merrimack Rivers* still captures an appealing sense of the place in days before human encroachment. In his early biography of Thoreau, Henry Seidel Canby wrote, "No river, not even the Thames, has been more lovingly, more accurately observed and interpreted than were the Concord and Sudbury by him." The views up and down the river are tranquil and inviting, making one wish for a canoe or kayak, or even for the wooden skiff Thoreau and his brother built and paddled upriver toward New Hampshire.

Beyond the river you come to a junction with MA 4 and arrive in Bedford, then *go right and west* at a tiny, pie-shaped green on MA 62 in the direction of West Bedford and Concord.

Pass the Church of St. Michael, Davis Road, and Warren Avenue, continuing west in a residential area and going by some marshy ground to the left at 1.6 miles. Cross the Concord line at 2.2 miles, keeping right at a junction by Pine Tree Farmstand at 2.8 miles. Now watch carefully on the right for Monsen Street, which, a mile and a half east of Concord center, leads you through a residential neighborhood and into a visitors area within Great Meadows NWR. Take time to stop here, climb the observation tower, and gaze over the marsh. A well-marked walking path will take you for a stroll around two large impounded ponds, which are (in season) very busy with the arrivals and departures of all manner of avian species. Muskrats build lodges here, and just above the ponds, the Concord River makes a series of serpentine bends through the woods.

MA 62 continues into the center of Concord, *making a left* in town and rounding the green *to the left* by the Colonial Inn at 4.3 miles. Immediately *go right* on Main Street in the center of town for one block where you *turn left* again and go southeast on Walden Street. This road drops toward Lincoln through a neighborhood of distinguished older residences, including the Ralph Waldo Emerson House at 4.7 miles. Walden Street makes a junction with Thoreau Street, passes the Concord-Carlisle Regional High School at 5.5 miles, and then *crosses* MA 2 and 2A, the Concord Turnpike.

Just beyond Routes 2 and 2A is the Walden Pond State Reservation, including a re-creation of Thoreau's legendary cabin, while to the right lies Walden Pond itself. Young Henry slipped away from the more settled precincts of Concord in 1845 to built his snug little cabin here, and moved in on July 4 of that year. He set about exploring the advantages of a simple life, writing it all down in shoals of introspective detail that emerged a decade later, in 1854, as *Walden*. His musings on the environment, on civil society, and on the role of the individual in community life have all proven both prophetic and valuable, and his diary of days spent here, timeless. The new Thoreau Institute in Lincoln (open by appoint-

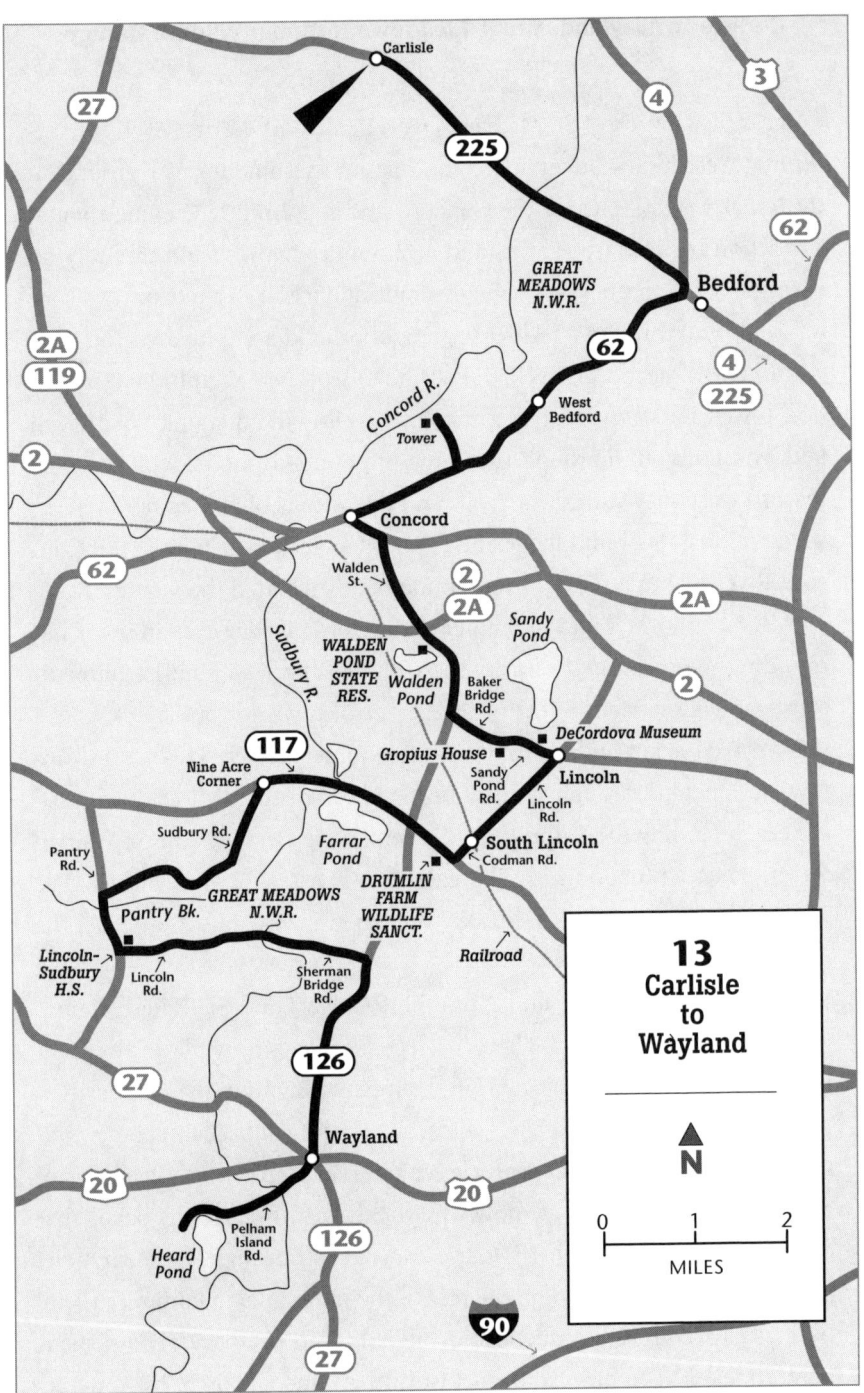

Carlisle

27

3

4

225

62

2A
119

GREAT
MEADOWS
N.W.R.

Bedford

West
Bedford

4
225

2

62

Concord R.

Tower

Concord

Walden
St.

2
2A

2A

Sudbury R.

*Sandy
Pond*

2

WALDEN
POND STATE
RES.

*Walden
Pond*

Baker
Bridge
Rd.

DeCordova Museum

117

Nine Acre
Corner

Gropius House

Sandy
Pond
Rd.

Lincoln

Lincoln
Rd.

Sudbury Rd.

*Farrar
Pond*

South Lincoln

Pantry
Rd.

GREAT MEADOWS
N.W.R.

Codman Rd.

Pantry Bk.

DRUMLIN
FARM
WILDLIFE
SANCT.

Lincoln-
Sudbury
H.S.

Lincoln
Rd.

Sherman
Bridge
Rd.

Railroad

27

126

Wayland

20

20

Pelham
Island
Rd.

126

*Heard
Pond*

90

27

**13
Carlisle
to
Wayland**

▲
N

0   1   2

MILES

 Great Meadows National Wildlife Refuge, Concord

ment), operated by the Thoreau Society, is a fine research and materials center for Thoreau enthusiasts.

Cross the Lincoln town line at 6.3 miles and roll through dense mixed pine and hardwood forest to Baker Bridge Road, where you *go left* toward Lincoln center in a corridor of hardwoods bordering Lincoln Conservation Association fields. I have been lucky enough to spot soaring hawks and owls here on more than one occasion. The road pulls northeast and, on the right, passes the white Gropius House at 7.4 miles. Built in 1937 and now operated by the Society for the Preservation of New England Antiquities, the house contains original furniture designed by Marcel Breuer and is one of the important earlier monuments to the influence of the Bauhaus style on residential architecture in America.

Go by the Carroll School at 7.9 miles, and then *bear right* around some pastureland onto Sandy Pond Road and shortly, on the left, you pass the

DeCordova Museum. A distinguished private museum whose collections reflect a range of modern periods and styles, the DeCordova also serves as a center for art education. A summer music series takes place in the amphitheater, and a network of walking trails visits nearby Sandy Pond. Inquire at the museum to find out about seasonal programs, exhibitions, and special events.

At 8.8 miles, you *turn right* by an old iron horse fountain and pass the Lincoln Town Offices and the white-colonnaded offices of Cottage Press as you go southwest on Lincoln Road. Roll into Lincoln's tiny shopping district, pass St. Joseph's Church and the village shops, cross the rail line, and then *keep left and southeast* on Codman Road. At 10.8 miles, *go right and west* on MA 117 (South Great Road). At 11.1 miles, round Massachusetts Audubon Society headquarters and parking for the Drumlin Farm Education Center and Wildlife Sanctuary, a must-visit site for anyone interested in natural history, animal husbandry, and farming. There are frequent special programs for children here.

Continue west on MA 117 in wooded residential country, cross MA 126 and enjoy views of rangy Farrar Pond on the left, which drains toward the Sudbury River at its western end. The route follows the pond's northern shore at 12.5 miles, crosses the Sudbury River at 13.2 miles, and skirts another section of the Great Meadows National Wildlife Refuge as it comes to Nine Acre Corners. From the Corners, *turn left* next onto Sudbury Road at 13.6 miles. This street drops south in a residential area west of the refuge, and then crosses the Sudbury town line, where it becomes Concord Road. It drifts more westward along the intriguing swampy margins of wandering Pantry Brook, passes a cluster of homes and meets Pantry Road at 16.1 miles, where you *go left and south.*

You cross over Pantry Brook now and continue south near the western perimeter of the Great Meadows reservation. Extensive rangy marshland on the left gradually yields to woodland, and at Lincoln-Sudbury Regional High School (17 miles) you *bear left and east* on pine-sheltered

Lincoln Road. This road hikes right into the heart of this more southerly section of the NWR, following some low stone walls along fields bordered by thick woods. At 18.4 miles watch on the left for Weir Hill Road, a marked lane providing entrance to the visitor center and the trail network in this part of the refuge. This area of the NWR makes a fine place to walk, enjoy the woods, and observe wildlife year-round. Trails circle a kettle hole and a red maple swamp. This place can be a blissful outdoor escape from the confines of the city on a hot summer day.

You'll cross the Sherman Bridge over the Sudbury River at 19.2 miles. Proceed farther east here on what is now Sherman Bridge Road to a junction with MA 126, Concord Road, at just under 20 miles. *Bear right and south* on MA 126. You now stay east of, but more or less parallel to, the Sudbury River and the NWR as you head down the map to Wayland. The road winds southwest and south in a rural residential zone with occasional patches of thick hardwoods. Pass Plain Road at 21.9 miles as you come into Wayland center and arrive at a major intersection with US 20 by the Wayland Library at 22.3 miles.

This rally round Great Meadows ends here, but you may want to tack a local destination onto your trip. Just west of this intersection, take Pelham Island Road southwest from US 20 for a mile and a half to Heard Pond, the southernmost body of water of any size in the NWR. This drive provides pleasing views as the road skirts the north side of the pond. 🦌

14

Route
Fitchburg to Townsend
Harbor, Lunenburg

Highway
MA 12, 101, 119, South Street,
Warren Road, Townsend Harbor Road

Distance
28 miles

Here is an interesting drive in the north-central zone of Massachusetts
near the New Hampshire border. The route forms a tight, inverted horse-
shoe in rural communities north of Fitchburg, southwest of Nashua, and
west of urban Lowell-Lawrence. A highlight of this drive is a meander
through Willard Brook State Forest, a wooded, hilly enclave of exceptional beauty where there are opportunities for streamside picnicking and
walking. The route also provides convenient access to more outdoor ram-
bles in nearby wildlife and state forest reservations.

This route begins at the junction of MA 2A and 12 a couple of miles
west of Fitchburg center. *Take MA 12*, which winds northwest out of
town through a residential area of older houses. At 1.2 miles the stone
wall–bordered route begins emerging into more rural terrain and the
houses thin out. Hop over the Westminster town line at 1.9 miles. This

route, sometimes called the Mid-State Trail by locals, rounds Potato Hill and crosses Phillips Brook at 2.4 miles while proceeding in the direction of Ashburnham, Massachusetts, and Keene, New Hampshire. Farther northwest, you enter Ashburnham township at 4.1 miles, pass Whitney Hill Road, then roll through Blackburn Village. You cross and re-cross Phillips Brook in this section, go over Brown Brook, and then skirt a pond (really a widening here of Phillips Brook). Come into the pleasant town center of Ashburnham at just under 6 miles, where you *bear right and north* on MA 101 by the Stevens Library, heading toward Ashby.

The road leaves Ashburnham in a cluster of older homes and climbs slightly north-northeast, following Phillips Brook, which now lies to the right. You're soon out in densely wooded country. In the Wellville section of Ashburnham, at nearly 8 miles, you pass pretty Winnekeag Lake on the left, backed by appealing views of Little Watatic Mountain in silhouette to the northwest. The road drifts northeast, passes a children's camp at 8.6 miles, goes by a partially submerged marsh on the right, and soon brushes Ward Pond, arriving at a junction with MA 119 at 10.3 miles. To the left and northwest is 1,800-foot Mount Watatic. (A narrow local road climbs the mountain from a point about a mile and a half west of here.)

Go right and east on MA 119 to continue, immediately leaving Worcester County for Middlesex County and passing Pillsbury Road on the left, which gives access to the densely wooded Ashby Wildlife Management Area. You'll have fine views north and south over water here. Drive by West Road, on the left, which also leads to the wildlife management area and on into New Hampshire via NH 123A. Continue east through sparsely settled rural country bordered by marshy lowlands and groves of hardwoods. Proceed through more rolling terrain to the little crossroads of Ashby. Pass the Ashby Fire Department at 13.3 and then the Town Offices amidst a number of attractive older buildings near the green. Heading farther east, you soon reenter wooded country and then continue east

The Most Scenic Roads in Massachusetts

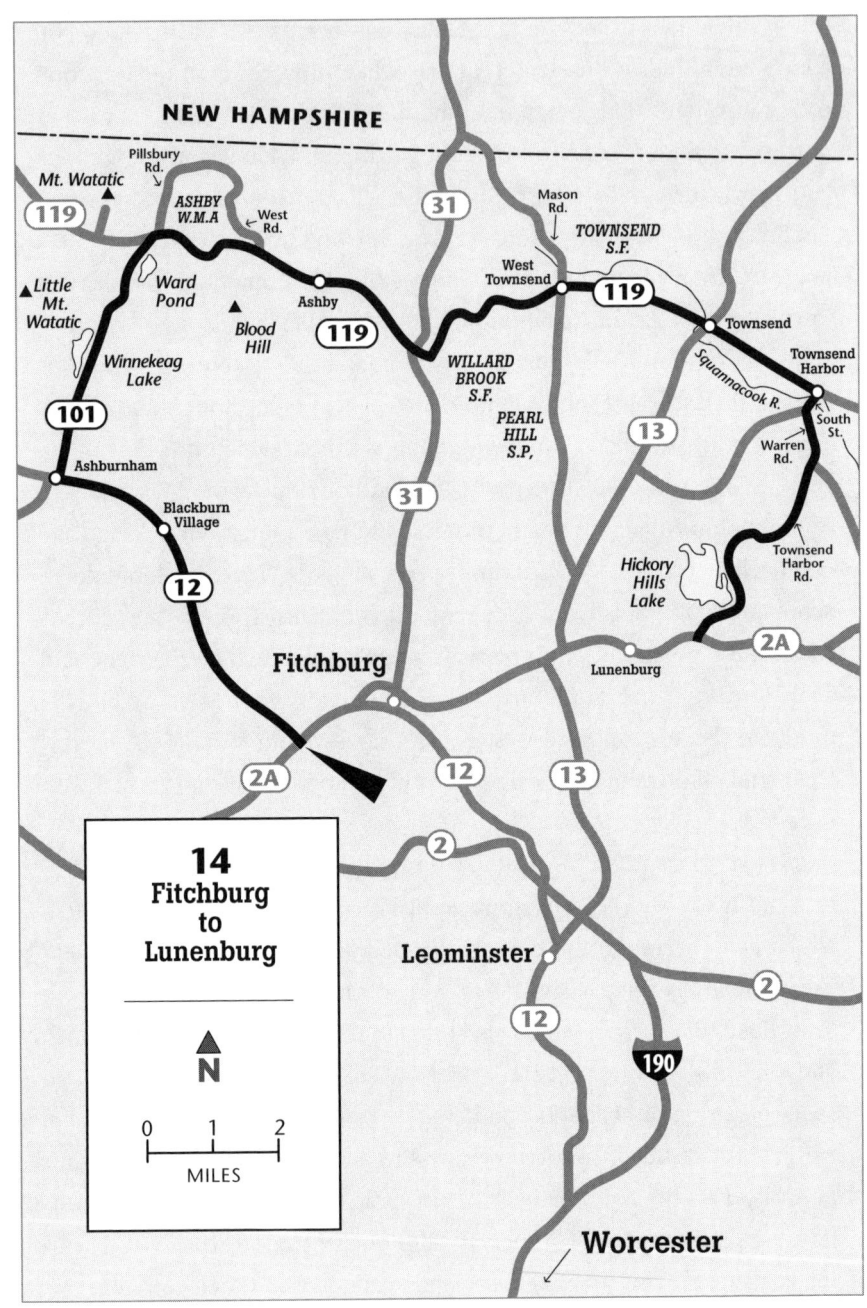

NEW HAMPSHIRE

Mt. Watatic

Pillsbury Rd.

ASHBY W.M.A

West Rd.

119

Little Mt. Watatic

Ward Pond

Ashby

Blood Hill

119

Winnekeag Lake

101

Ashburnham

Blackburn Village

12

31

31

WILLARD BROOK S.F.

PEARL HILL S.P.

13

Mason Rd.

TOWNSEND S.F.

West Townsend

119

Townsend

Townsend Harbor

Squannacook R.

Warren Rd.

South St.

Townsend Harbor Rd.

Hickory Hills Lake

Fitchburg

2A

Lunenburg

2A

12

13

2

Leominster

12

2

190

Worcester

**14
Fitchburg
to
Lunenburg**

N

0 1 2
MILES

to where 119 meets MA 31 at 15.4 miles. Now you'll *turn left* on 31 and then *go immediately right*, staying on MA 119.

Here you begin the prettiest section of this drive, following the lands of Willard Brook State Forest as you trend northeast. This exceptional forest preserve is dense with conifers, particularly great, tall hemlocks, and the road hugs attractive Willard Brook to the right. There are a number of inviting places to picnic at brookside along here and a camping area featuring twenty-one campsites and rustic cabin accommodations. A trail network provides access to Trapp Falls and to swimming at Damon Pond. Side roads explore the interior of the forestlands. It's truly a beautiful place.

Willard Brook has worn its way between two adjacent hills, and the whole area has an enchanting primeval quality to it — something unexpected so close to several major metropolitan centers. It's very much worth the time to take a break here and walk forest trails or explore the river bank.

You come to the Townsend line at 17 miles and pass the state forest headquarters, then drop northeast into low country fed by Walker Brook and the Squannacook River, where there are broad, open fields and marshes to the left as you come into West Townsend. At 18.7 miles, watch for Old Battery Road or West Elm Street on the right, both of which lead south to Pearl Hill State Park. You'll find further opportunities for hiking and camping there. Also in the town center, Mason Road jumps north over the Squannacook to a side street leading into expansive Townsend State Forest, another appealing woodland open to exploration.

Going over a rail line on MA 119, you come next to Townsend, where you cross the broad Squannacook and go through a junction with MA 13. MA 119 stays with the river, now to your right, as you come into Townsend Harbor by attractive Harbor Pond. Drive by the Townsend Historical Society's interesting Reed Homestead at 22.9 miles.

Just beyond the pond and homestead you *bear right and south* onto

South Street by the gristmill and the old Conant Tavern, and then *left* on Warren Road at 23.3 miles. This street winds through a residential area and then plays tag with Trout Brook in less-settled low country. After crossing Trout Brook, the route becomes Townsend Harbor Road as it runs southwest through some low, boggy terrain, passes stone walls, and crosses into the township of Lunenburg in Worcester County at 26 miles.

The drive winds down now as it reaches the northeast shore of rangy Hickory Hills Lake, follows the east shore of the lake, and then rolls along the shore to the southwest, where you may slow for excellent views to northward over a high berm at the water's edge. Round the lake and pull away from the shore at 27.4 miles, crossing Mulpus Brook, which feeds an impressive mile-long marsh to the southeast. Just beyond, you come to the junction of Townsend Harbor Road and MA 2A in Lunenburg, where this route concludes at just under 28 miles. From here, you may go right on 2A to reach Fitchburg or turn left and east for West Groton and (via MA 111) the town of Ayer 🦌.

15

Route
Leicester to Phillipston
Highway
MA 56, 31, 62, 68, Williamsville Road,
MA 101, Barre Road, Baldwinville Road
Distance
46 miles

Here is a quiet backcountry drive that climbs northward through rural communities west of Worcester and the great Wachusett Reservoir. Taking in small settlements like Paxton, Holden, Princeton, and Hubbardston, the route ascends to tiny Phillipston village in north-central Massachusetts, near Athol. Though it begins not far from bustling Worcester, this drive drifts away from industrialized corners of the Bay State to explore country that might well be in New Hampshire or Maine, so rural is its character. Constructed out of both numbered highways and wandering local roads, this route will often take you onward for miles without seeing another car.

This excursion begins west of Worcester in the small town of Leicester, a place settled centuries ago by immigrants from the English midlands city of the same name. Take off from the junction of MA 9 and MA 56 by the police station in the center of Leicester, and *go north* on 56 in

 Winter at the green, Princeton

the direction of Paxton. *Stay left* by the attractive town green and the campus of Becker College and then pass Leicester High School. The road quickly becomes rural, and at 1.5 miles starts climbing upward through high fields west of Worcester Municipal Airport. Some very fine, high outlooks to the east open up here. You reenter heavily forested lands and, on the right at 2.1 miles, will pass the first of a series of ponds and reservoirs you'll see on this route. Not far beyond, you cross into Paxton (2.7 miles) and, on the left, skirt a long, north-south pond that catches outflow from Kettle Brook Reservoir Number 4. You pull away from the pond in hardwoods and a border of red pines but then soon have views of the reservoir itself on the left.

Come to a T intersection, where you *stay left* on MA 56 and MA 122, going northwest and rolling by a pretty marsh. Pass the Paxton Dispatch

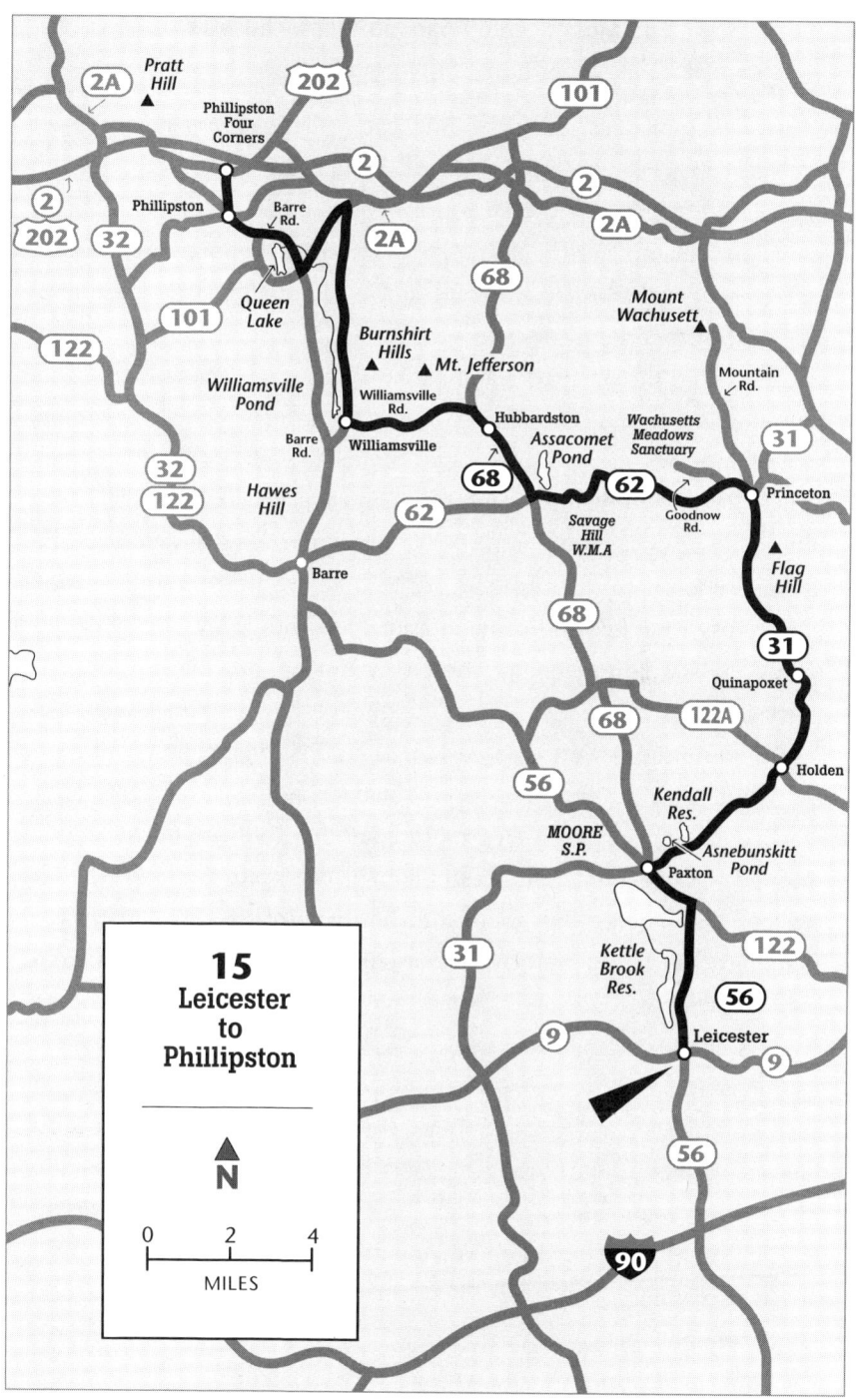

2A   Pratt Hill ▲   202

101

Phillipston Four Corners

2

2

2A

2   Phillipston   Barre Rd.   2A

202   32

68

Mount Wachusett ▲

101   Queen Lake

Mountain Rd.

122

Burnshirt Hills ▲   ▲ Mt. Jefferson

Williamsville Pond

Williamsville Rd.

Hubbardston

Wachusetts Meadows Sanctuary

31

32   Barre Rd.   Williamsville

68

Assacomet Pond

62

Savage Hill W.M.A

Goodnow Rd.

Princeton

122   Hawes Hill

62   Barre

Flag Hill ▲

68

31

Quinapoxet

68   122A

56   Holden

Kendall Res.

MOORE S.P.   Asnebunskitt Pond

Paxton

122

31

Kettle Brook Res.

56

9   Leicester   9

56

90

15
Leicester to Phillipston

▲ N

0   2   4

MILES

Center at 4.7 miles, as you come into Paxton village. (If you are interested in a side trip, a left on MA 31 at 5.2 miles will bring you to nearby Moore State Park.) By the attractive Paxton common and St. Columba's Church, leave MA 122 and *go right and northeast* on MA 31 toward Holden. *Take another right* by the Richards Library, *staying east* on MA 31 (Maple Street) where MA 56 continues north. At a T, MA 31 also goes north briefly, emerging into the open with hill views of giant antenna farms on surrounding highlands. Bending eastward, you cross the Holden town line at 6.9 miles in boggy, spruce- and hemlock-spotted ground in thick groves of oak, and then go around Asnebunskitt Pond on the left. In another mile or so you have grand water views over Kendall Reservoir and its outflow on both sides of the road. Pass Reservoir Street at 8.8 miles. Next, cross a rail line and come to a junction with MA 122A by the attractive First Congregational Church in Holden, where you continue northeast on 31 past the old stone building of the Gale Free Library.

Climb northeastward next on MA 31 in a residential area and cross the Quinapoxet River at just over 12 miles as the terrain gets more wooded. You move past rolling pasture and horses in paddocks at 14.2 miles, then crest a hill and descend along stone walls. Cross Princeton's town line at 15 miles while rolling due north in isolated rural terrain. The route next skirts Flag Hill, rising to a point where there are continuous spectacular views to the east. On a crystal clear day, one might see nearly all the way to Boston from here.

You arrive at an intersection with MA 62 opposite the sloping hillside green in Princeton village at 18 miles. (An interesting side trip to nearby Mount Wachusett, one of the Bay State's higher elevations, may be made by following Mountain Road, which rises ahead to the north and up the hill by the church. The Mount Wachusett Reservation is roughly 3 miles above the common.)

To continue this journey, you'll *go left and west* on MA 62 here. Shortly you come to Goodnow Road on the right, which will take you to Massachusetts Audubon's Wachusett Meadows Wildlife Sanctuary—worth a visit. Then roll on through open country, passing pretty Fieldstone Farm at almost 20 miles. More stone walls border the road here, backed by a low, wooded ridgeline to the west. Cross South Wachusett Brook and then cross a rail line in a neighborhood known as Princeton Station. You roll past a tiny pond at 21.2 miles and then follow a low bogland for some distance, eventually crossing its source, the East Branch of the Ware River, as you go by the Savage Hill Wildlife Management Area to the left. Go over the Hubbardston town line just beyond, at 23.3 miles. In less than a mile you'll pass fine views of lovely Assacomet Pond on the right and come to an intersection with MA 68. *Go right and north* now on broader MA 68, toward Hubbardston center.

The road north heads through mixed-growth forest banked back from the pavement, the woods opening soon to reveal pleasing outlooks over attractive Brighton Pond to the east. Climbing next at 26.3 miles, you ascend into Hubbardston center, the road lined here with older period homes. Now you really take to the backcountry. At 27.5 miles, beyond the fire station, *go left and west* on the Williamsville Road, which dips past a couple of farms and into an area of marshy ground, where it crosses Natty Pond Brook. Off to the right is 1,200-foot Mount Jefferson. There also are good views ahead to the ridgeline of the Burnshirt Hills as you proceed along low stone walls, descending and climbing alternately. Crossing Canesto Brook, *go right and north* at a T intersection onto Burnshirt Road (31.7 miles) near the interesting old Williamsville Chapel, a white-clapboard structure set here in 1888.

To the left there are water views of long, thin Williamsville Pond as you roll north now through densely wooded terrain. The road widens to parkway dimensions, and the Burnshirt Hills loom to the right as you roll over the Templeton town line at 32.7 miles. Here, fine, long views prevail to the left and to hills far ahead, and you come in minutes to a T with MA 101 at 36.7 miles. *Go left and west* here, toward Petersham. Descend past several fields into woods on a decidedly rougher road. Then, on a winding up-and-down stretch, pass through a lowland connected to the Burnshirt River and rise past high, rolling pasture at Fox Hollow Farm (38.4 miles), crossing into Phillipston just beyond.

The route passes more horses in paddocks here at Stone Brook Stable and then hops over another brook, with views rightward to a hauntingly pretty marsh within the Phillipston Wildlife Management Area. At 38.9 miles you *turn right* on the Barre Road, following signs for Phillipston Center. You now run alongside the wildlife area you first saw a moment ago. Here it's a broad and imposing raised peat bog of considerable size, an unspoiled, wild-looking place. You next pull westward around the top of scenic Queen Lake and reach a junction where, on the left, Searles Hill Road joins Barre Road. A few yards on, amidst a network of old stone walls, you arrive at the pretty little common of Phillipston at 41.1 miles. A school and the Phillipston Congregational Church overlook the green. This quiet settlement was founded in 1786, and the church congregation preceded it by a year.

From the common, *go north* now on the Baldwinville Road, passing the Athol Road on your left, as you head out of the village toward Phillipston Four Corners. On the Baldwinville Road you descend through woodlands off the high mound you've been on and cross tiny Dunn Brook, coming to a junction with MA 2A at 46 miles, where this drive ends. From here, MA 2A leads right and east a short distance to MA 2 and Templeton, or west to Athol. ⚑

16

Route

Southbridge-Sturbridge Loop

Highway

MA 131, South Street, Mashapaug Road, I-84,
Mashapaug Road, Brimfield Road,
New Holland Road, US 20, Monson Road,
Dean Pond Road, Sutcliff Road, Mount Hitchcock Road,
McBride Road, Monson Road, MA 19,
New Holland Road, Five Bridge Road, US 20

Distance

36.3 miles

This leisurely backroads exploration of Massachusetts's south-central border country visits an antiques center, loops around several lakes, doubles back on itself, and concludes at the site of famous Old Sturbridge Village. Along the way, the drive heads right through beautiful Brimfield State Forest, crosses a major deadwater, and touches a number of places ideal for camping and recreational activities. If a healthy mix of rural back roads and attractive woodlands suits you, and you have a penchant for things antique, travel these roads.

Begin in the south central city of Southbridge at the junction of MA 169 and MA 131 on the east side of town. *Go west,* crossing the down-

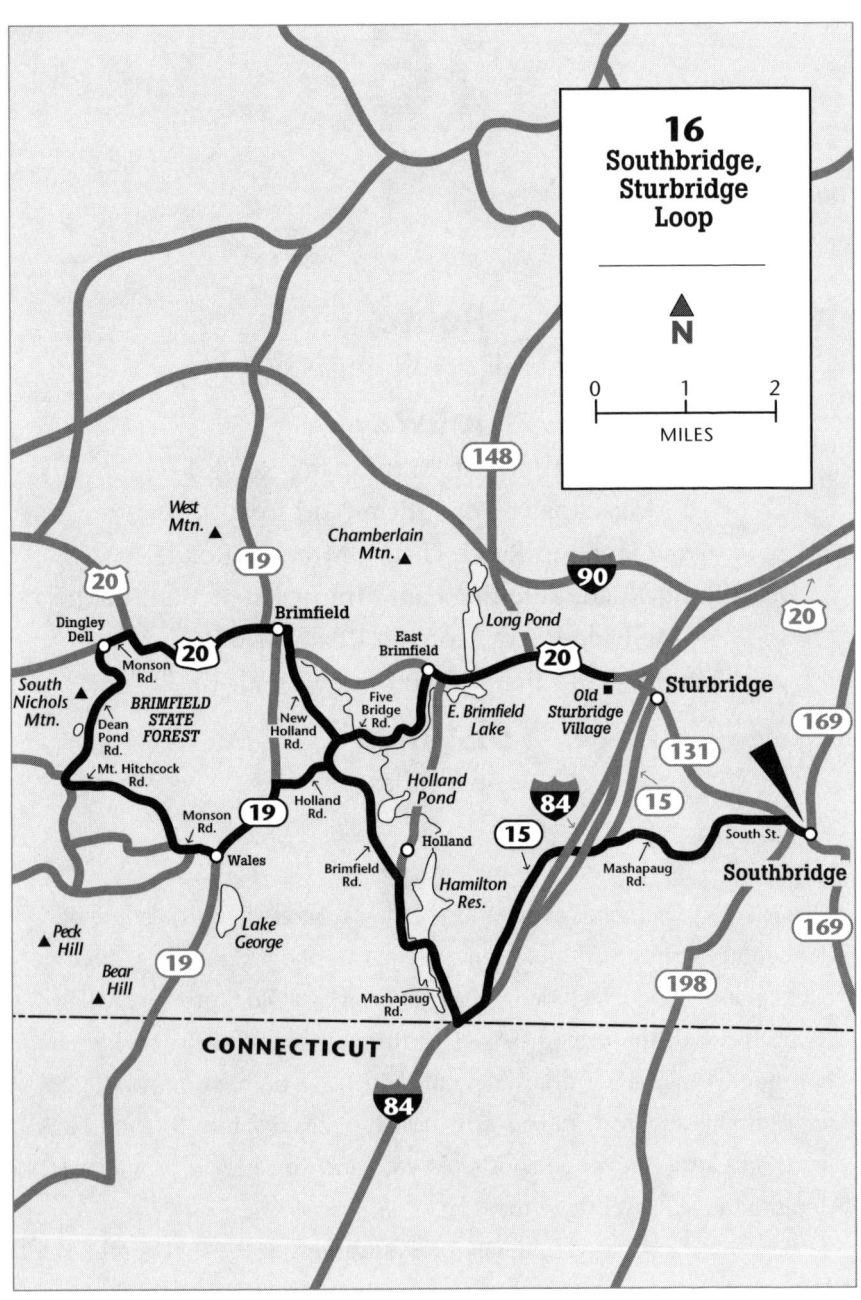

16
Southbridge,
Sturbridge
Loop

N

0   1   2
MILES

town area on 131, and watch for South Street on the left by Notre Dame Church a half mile from your starting point. *Turn left* on South Street at a fork. South Street passes through a residential area and is soon out in more rural terrain, rolling by a widened, pondlike section of the Quinebaug River to the right. Beyond Breakneck Road, South Street shortly becomes Mashapaug Road at 2.7 miles and pulls west through more wooded country. Drive through several rock cuts and gain altitude, some views to the north opening up shortly. At 3.6 miles you cross a deadwater, and the road winds south in mixed-growth forest, soon coming to a T at Interstate 84 and MA 15. *Go left* on MA 15 and *under* I-84 and head south for several miles as quiet, untrafficked MA 15 parallels busy I-84 and then joins it briefly at 7.7 miles. The country around MA 15 is densely wooded and undeveloped, with occasional views to low hills off to the left. The combined MA 15 and I-84 cross a few hundred yards into Tolland County, Connecticut, where you *leave* I-84 on the right at Exit 74 in Mashapaug. Follow the exit road *west* a stone's throw to unmarked Mashapaug Road and then *go left and northwest* toward Holland and Brimfield.

Mashapaug Road drops north in a residential section backed by a marshy area and an arm of Hamilton Reservoir to the left at 8.5 miles. Views leftward improve as you go north and get closer to the reservoir with wooded upland to the right. (The route is variously marked Holland Road and Old Mashapaug Road in this poorly signed section. Stay on the main road.) At just over 10 miles the road pulls left and northwest, navigating a causeway that offers splendid views up and down the reservoir, and then turns north again. Numerous points offer excellent outlooks over the reservoir to the right now as you climb the map to Holland, with a range of hills providing a backdrop to the broad upper lake. At 10.9 miles there is a turnout by a boat launch overlooking the widest point in the reservoir.

Keep left at a fork in Holland at 11.5 miles, going northwest on the

Brimfield Road. The route now follows a vast, low, marshy area to the right fed by Mill Brook and the Quinebaug. This is wooded, rural country bordered by tall white pines. Go by Pond Bridge Road on the right at 12.9 miles and roll along in mixed-growth forest with views of low hills to the north ahead. You leap the Quinebaug River soon and, at 14.2 miles, cross the Brimfield town line with Five Bridge Road on the right and high, lovely pasture to your left. Remember this little side road; you'll be coming back this way.

Brimfield Road becomes New Holland Road now, as you continue north, cross Wales Brook, and come to an intersection with US 20 (at 16.2 miles) on a broad, sweeping bend in Brimfield. *Go left* cautiously here on US 20, pass through a junction with MA 19, and meander west through Brimfield past the long Brimfield Common and the delightful Victorian town hall. Brimfield is one of the great antiques centers of New England. Numerous dealer pavilions line the road, and in May, July, and September, antiques dealers and fanciers from all over the northeast descend on this spot to buy and sell. If you adore antiques, it's hard to get by here in those months without a lengthy visit. At 18 miles, continue toward hill country to the southwest and then west, now in lovely rural countryside. Pass a standing deadwater on the right as the hills close in on both sides while the road climbs around West Mountain, the long shape of which lies off to the right.

At 19.4 miles, watch for the well-signed entrance for Brimfield State Forest where you *turn left* off US 20 and head southwest on Monson Road in thick mixed-growth woods. There are fine hill views left and right ahead to North and South Nichols Mountain here in scattered stands of white birch. Cross Foskett Mill Stream at just over 20 miles and, at a crossroads known as Dingley Dell, shortly *bear left and south* on Dean Pond Road, where you head into the state forest in lovely groves of hemlocks on a narrow pavement.

The road drops south through extraordinarily pretty forest and bog-

Dean Pond, Brimfield

land and arrives at the outlet of attractive Dean Pond at 21.8 miles. Park and climb the path up the berm so you can gaze across this serene little pond nestled beneath a hillside to the west. Just beyond, as you head south, is the entrance to the Dean Pond Recreation Area. Operated by the Massachusetts Department of Environmental Management, it is an excellent seasonal destination. This route is now known as Sutcliff Road as you proceed southward and pass a campground and picnic area, arriving at a T intersection at 23.1 miles, where you *go left* on Mount Hitchcock Road.

You now cross into the town of Wales at 23.7 miles and climb to the east in and out of state forestlands. There are occasional outlooks from this high ground as you proceed up through stands of hardwoods bordered by stone walls, pass Tiderman Road, and then descend through some attractive farm pastures. *Go left* again on winding McBride Road, which joins Old Monson Road at 26.3 miles, and follow Monson Road due east to Wales. You pass a sweet little pond and brook with hill views off to the north at 26.6 miles, and then cross another brook a few hundred yards farther on. Both the pond and the brooks feed Lake George nearby to the south. At 27 miles you come to a T with MA 19 in Wales by the Wales Baptist Church and Oak Haven Campground.

Heading left and north on MA 19, you pass the Wales Elementary School and then an old stone horse fountain of the type every rural community had a century ago. On the right, you follow Wales Brook for a mile and a half, *going right* on Holland Road at 28.4 miles. The route here is densely wooded and rural, a marsh appearing on the left that accommodates a tributary of Wales Brook. After climbing a hill, you cross into Holland and the road narrows and becomes a little rough. Go by Wales Road and continue northeast past rough, granite-strewn ground and hardwood forest to a cluster of houses at 29.9 miles. Just beyond, reach a junction with New Holland Road, which you rode northward earlier.

Go north and left again here for a short distance, crossing the Brimfield town line for a second time at 30.3 miles. Immediately on the right, spot Five Bridge Road on which you will *bear right and northeast*. Just as quickly you are back in wilder country, the visual fare now being the vast north-south Mill Brook flowage. Slow here for interesting views up and down this wild, golden marshland as you cross Mill Brook at 30.8 miles. The road now reenters woods but clings to the very edge of the great marsh to the south, staying with it for over a mile. Marshgrass and bent spotted alder yields to oak and pine here in cover inhabited by ringnecked pheasant and whitetail deer. Continuing northeast, you reach some scattered houses at 32.4 miles and roll along stone walls backed by fine outlooks over hills and valleys to the right, with horses and cattle in hillside fields.

At 32.9 miles, you reach US 20 once again. This time *go right and east*, trading the intense quiet of the network of back roads just traversed for this busy highway. There are rewards here, nonetheless, as you enjoy fine views to the right and left of beautiful East Brimfield Lake, one section of which you follow for some distance, passing the waterfront Streeter Point Recreation Area. With hill views to the north, you cross from Hampden into Worcester County, go through a junction with MA 148, and continue east on 20 (now in Sturbridge), going by the East Brimfield Dam at 34.2 miles. Leaving woods, lakes, and hills behind, you shortly come into a rather overdeveloped area of Sturbridge. Passing through a district of shops, restaurants, and accommodations, you reach the end of this drive at the entrance to Old Sturbridge Village at 36.3 miles.

Old Sturbridge Village admits one, for a fee, to the vanished world of a circa-1820 New England town. The 20-acre complex features new and restored period architecture, demonstrations, costumed "citizens" larking about, and other artifacts of yesteryear. Some thought has gone into this well-established exhibit, and it certainly provides the visitor with an engaging and interesting reconnection with early American life in an authentic way that places like the expensive Disneybore don't. The Village, which at times can be very crowded, is open to visitors daily from April to December and on weekends or a part-week schedule the rest of the year. Attractive overnight accommodations are available on site. ⚓

17

Route
Hingham, Scituate, Duxbury, Plymouth
Highway
MA 3A, 80, 44, Carver Street, Summer Street
Distance
35 miles

When Bostonians head out to "the Cape," they tend to clamber aboard MA 3, turn south, and put a brick on the accelerator. On a summer day, there may be a certain virtue in getting well down the South Shore as quickly as physics allow, but there are more congenial alternatives. MA 3A links Boston and the Cape, but as a *local* road offering exposure to many of the small towns that dot the South Shore. As payment for time spent in those settled areas that sometimes dominate, MA 3A also treats the traveler to woodland, marsh, river, and harbor views that are a pleasing alternative to hurtling south on its highway counterpart. Since this route collects coastal towns the way P. T. Barnum collected oddities, there's an almost continuous opportunity to slip into the center of the many villages passed, to visit local beaches, and to walk the shore as you will.

This route begins in the center of Hingham by the broad expanse of Hingham Harbor. Before setting out, you might want to first spend a little time at World's End, just to the north of the town center, on nearby

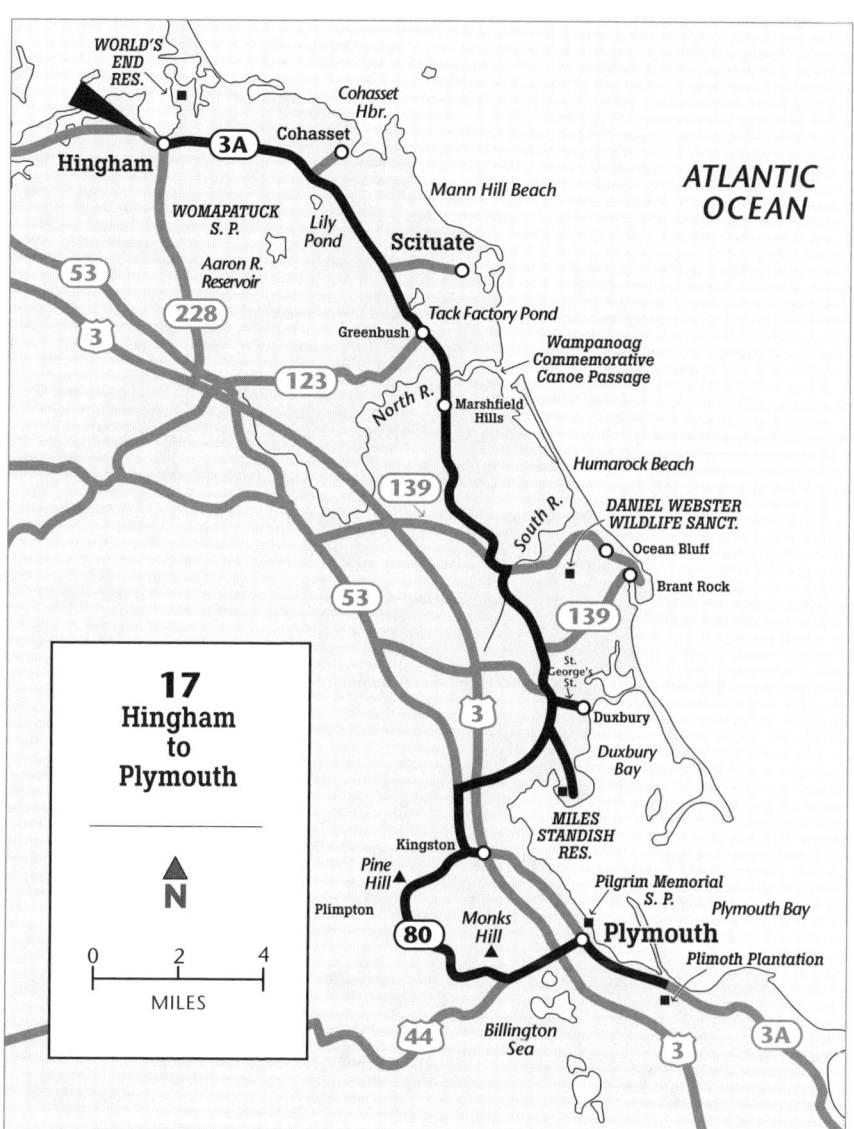

17
Hingham to Plymouth

N

0   2   4
MILES

Martins Lane. The World's End reservation provides a delightful place to walk amid natural surroundings designed by Frederick Law Olmsted and enjoy spectacular views across Hingham Bay to Boston Harbor (see the author's *Weekend Walks on the New England Coast*).

The Most Scenic Roads in Massachusetts

From the junction of Summer Street and MA 3A, at a rotary, *take 3A southeast and east* in the direction of Cohasset and Scituate. Pass Kirby and East Streets and, at 1.7 miles, go by an entrance to Wompatuck State Park, a large reservation where there is camping near Prospect Hill and Accord Brook. The Aaron River Reservoir also is located in the park. You cross MA 228 and then the Cohasset line in moments. The route gets quickly out into pretty marsh here to the south, an interesting contrast to the built-up neighborhood you just left behind. You skirt the Cohasset Knoll area as the road gets back into a built-up section, passing Sohier Street on the left, which connects with Cohasset center and Cohasset Harbor. Wending in and out of commercial neighborhoods, the road passes through a wooded area where Lily Pond lies off to the right.

You roll over the Scituate town line at 5 miles and enter Plymouth County. On the left an enormous coastal wetland stretches eastward toward Mann Hill Beach as you roll by hidden Bound Brook and then pass the Scituate Town Forest at 6.2 miles. Arborway Drive, to the left at 7.2 miles, leads to Scituate center. Continuing southeast on 3A, you shortly reach Lock Factory Pond and First Herring Brook, on the left and right, at 8 miles. Excellent water views appear briefly on both sides of the road. Go through a junction with MA 123 west in Greenbush and then emerge to wide marsh views east and west as you cross the North River at 9.9 miles. This riverine marsh is the entrance to the Wampanoag Commemorative Canoe Passage, linking the Atlantic with the historic Wampanoag territories to the southwest. The North River connects with the Indian Head River and Herring Brook, both of which reach west and south to networks of other streams, brooks, and ponds in the towns of Pembroke, Hanson, and Whitman.

The route next drops due south through Marshfield Hills, running parallel to the great salt marshes behind Humarock Beach, to the east, and passing the Massachusetts Audubon Society's North River Sanctuary. The road climbs slightly along a raised ridge (these are "hills" in name only) and then brushes by the Furnace Brook Conservation Area, on the right at 12.6 miles.

MA 3A next comes into a more built-up area, crosses the South River, and is joined by MA 139, which comes in from the right at 15.5 miles. The South River marshes lie to the left and east where the river opens to the sea behind Humarock Beach. MA 3A pulls away from 139 in just minutes, at 16 miles, where 139 goes east to the Daniel Webster Wildlife Sanctuary and on to Ocean Bluff and Brant Rock. Stay with 3A as it continues southeast toward Duxbury.

The road narrows and winds in a residential neighborhood that yields soon to low hardwoods in more rural country where there are cranberry harvesting operations. You enter Duxbury at 17.8 miles, soon coming to a section of attractive older houses, then crossing the Back River in low ground. At 19.5 miles you go by St. George's Street on the left, which will carry you into the center of Duxbury and to the grave of fabled Plymouth Colony father Captain Miles Standish. Duxbury village is also the site of the preserved home of Plymouth Colony's John Alden.

MA 3A pulls more to the southwest as you drive past a connector road to the left leading to Myles Standish State Reservation. (The reservation lies on the south end of Eagle Neck, surrounding Captain's Hill, and merits a side trip.) The route hops *over* MA 3 next, at 23 miles, and then, at a junction with MA 53, *goes left and south.* You drive south on 3A past a couple of ugly malls and then roll through a more appealing older residential neighborhood, working your way into the pleasant center of Kingston. Coming out of town through rows of old Victorians and Federals, you rise to a junction with MA 80 west, where you leave MA 3A and *bear right,* making a loop now through some pretty, wooded country to the west of Plymouth.

MA 80 crosses the serene Jones River Marsh and follows it southwest for a way. Going through a residential area close to Plympton, the road crests on the low hummock of Pine Hill and then pulls sharply southeast

 At Plymouth Rock

and south, descending through a series of ponds, with water outlooks to left and right at 26.6 miles. Going around Muddy Pond and Monks Hill to the left, MA 80 dips through pine woods and then turns sharply east at 27.7 miles as you cross the Plymouth town line. Submerged cranberry bogs spread out to the right here.

You reach a residential area and a golf course in stands of jack pines and white pines as you come into Plymouth center, reaching a junction where you *stay left. Keep left* again at a rotary opposite Sacred Heart High School just beyond, and then make still another *left* turn on MA 44. Watch for Carver Road on the south side of 44 in less than a mile, where you *keep right,* continuing southeast through a residential area to Summer Street. *Go left and due east* at 32.9 miles, on Summer Street, which will bring you right into the heart of historic Plymouth.

Summer Street descends toward the Plymouth waterfront along a stream that connects a sizable lake known as the Billington Sea with the ocean. You pass a mill pond and old gristmill site on the right, going by the old Sparrow House as you drift eastward into town. In moments you

Visitors center at Plimoth Plantation

come to a T with Plymouth's Main Street, where you *go left* for a couple of blocks in the shopping district. *Take the first available right* off the main shopping street onto Middle Street and emerge at famous Plymouth Rock by the statue of Massasoit, where this drive ends at 35. 4 miles. Follow signs for directions to parking areas.

Here's an opportunity to recollect the lessons of your grade-school history classes. From this high promontory, there are pleasant walks around the historic Plymouth Rock monument, to the Pilgrim Hall Museum, and through Plymouth's interesting downtown.

Plimoth Plantation, a modern-day re-creation of the original Plymouth settlement, lies 2 miles south of town, on MA 3A. Perusing a copy of William Bradford's *Of Plymouth Plantation, 1620–1647,* as edited by Samuel Eliot Morison, will add much to your understanding of Plymouth's role in the early colonization of New England.

18

Route
Fairhaven to Plymouth

Highway
Main Street, MA 105, 28, Rocky Gutter Street,
France Street, Popes Point Road, Meadow Street, MA 58,
Tremont Street, Cranberry Road, Barre Hill, Rocky Pond Road,
Watercourse, Billington Street, Summer Street

Distance
47 miles

Here is a drive that explores the backcountry between two of Massachusetts's most important South Shore cities. The route will carry you through the small towns north of Fairhaven and New Bedford, around the lake country south of Middleborough, and then east to Plymouth through the cranberry bogs and sublime woodlands of Carver and the Myles Standish State Forest. Much of the trip remains determinedly rural, often following narrow country roads very little traveled. This leisurely South Shore excursion through places of great beauty typically missed by travelers wedded to the major interstates will introduce you to a series of pleasant discoveries not far from Boston.

This route begins in Fairhaven, across the river from New Bedford. Before you drive north, historically rich Fairhaven and New Bedford should both be explored, if you are not familiar with them. Fairhaven is a community with long connections to the sea. Its Poverty Point area along the shores of the Acushnet River dates back to 1660, when John Cooke, a *Mayflower* traveler, built a garrison house there. The Poverty Point area still boasts several preserved old houses built before 1800. Shipbuilding had become an economic force here by 1710. During the Revolution, privateers operated aggressively out of New Bedford–Fairhaven waters from both sides of the Acushnet. Interesting Nolscot Point is the site of Fort Phoenix, first built in 1777 and rebuilt in 1783. The locally available *Visitors Guide to Fairhaven* makes a helpful companion, offering several walking tours that take in some of Fairhaven's most historically important sites.

Across the Acushnet is New Bedford, once the whaling capital of the world and today a busy fishing port. From cobblestoned Johnny Cake Hill, the old Whalemen's Bethel still casts its glance across the harbor as it did in the days evoked in Herman Melville's *Moby Dick*. A thirteen-block downtown area constitutes the New Bedford Whaling National Historic Park. The New Bedford Whaling Museum is home to the largest collection of whaling memorabilia in the world. Salty visitors can climb onto the deck of a half-scale, fully rigged whaling ship here. Other attractions such as the New Bedford Art Museum and the New Bedford Fire Museum are every bit worth visiting, as are the magnificent old houses clustered in the County Street area.

This drive leaves Fairhaven from the junction of Main Street and MA 6 just east of the bridge that crosses the Acushnet and Pope's Island, connecting Fairhaven with New Bedford. From the High School, a distinguished structure built in 1906 by oil millionaire Henry Huttleston Rogers, and the Museum of Fairhaven History, *follow Main Street north*, passing Oxford Street, and wind through an area of older homes in a neighborhood also known as Oxford. You then come to a junction with Alden Street in North Fairhaven. Here you cross into Acushnet, continu-

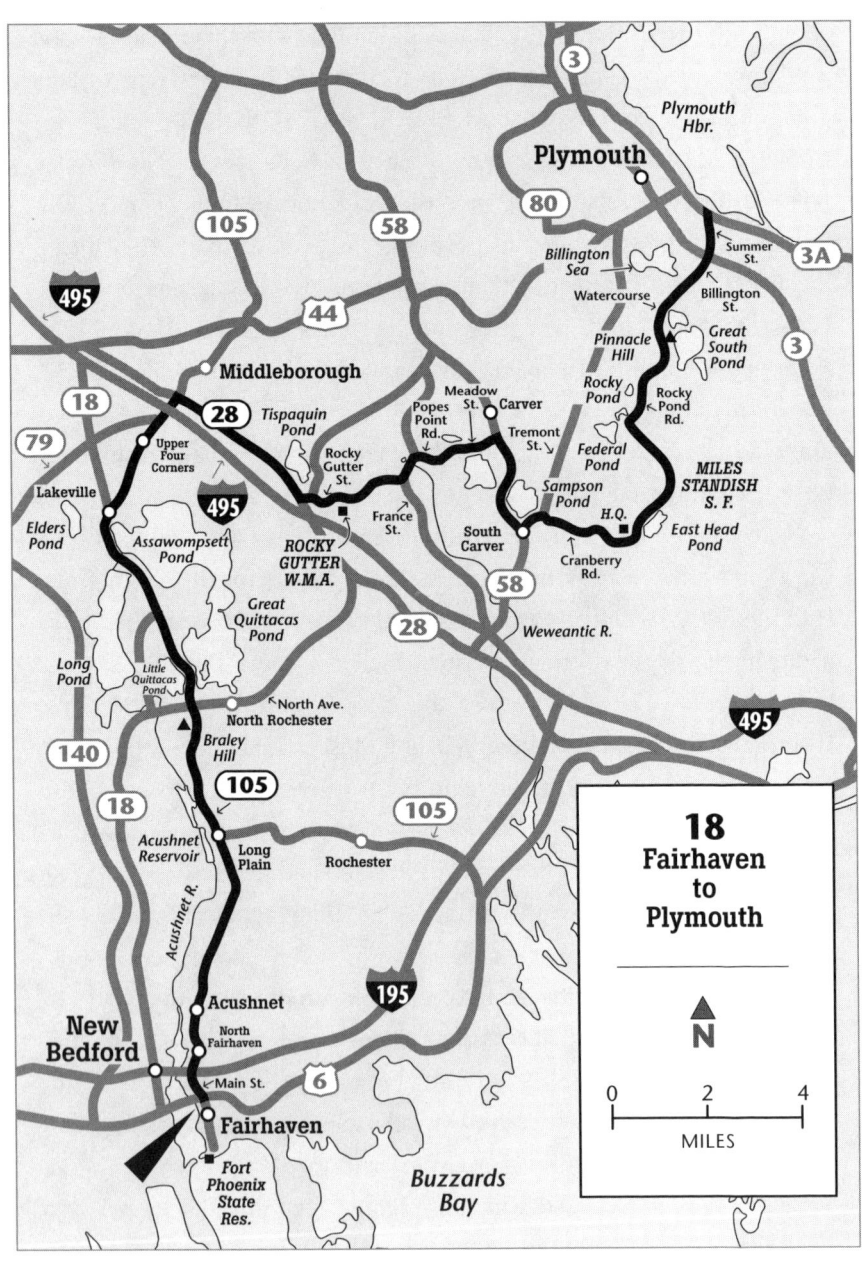

Southeastern sky and shore

ing north on Main. You now roll along by vine-covered stone walls and pass the Acushnet Town Hall on the common at 3 miles.

Beyond Acushnet, you are soon out in more open country as the road climbs northeast parallel to the Acushnet River amidst orchards and small farms. Views to the west open up at 5.4 miles, and you enter lines of old hard rock maples near Silver Brooks Farm at just over 6 miles. Main Street and MA 105 become one in the rural farmlands of Long Plain at 7.4 miles. Continuing farther north, you climb Braley Hill and cross into Plymouth County and the town of Rochester at 9.4 miles, passing a long, low woodland to the right known as the Logging Swamp.

Cross North Avenue and descend next to aptly named Lakeville, entering a pretty region of ponds formed by three bodies of water: Great Quittacas Pond and Little Quittacas Pond to the right and left and Assawompsett Pond farther along on the right. Views to Little Quittacas Pond are sublime, and a bog to the right soon yields to views of Great

Quittacas that verge on the idyllic. The greater pond is home to Little, Great, and Anuxanon Islands. You now pull northwest through groves of red pines, go through a junction with MA 18 and pass the Lakeville Historical Museum just beyond. There are more fine water views to the left and southwest as you next cross the broad, marshy land bridge that separates Assawompsett from a fourth body of water, Long Pond.

In a few minutes, you *bear right and northeast* on 105 in Lakeville Center at 16.2 miles, following 105 through open fields and scattered woodlands to Upper Four Corners at 18 miles. You move now through a more developed area as you continue northeast, pass under US 495, and come to a junction with MA 28 in Middleborough.

The country hereabouts was once the region of King Philip's War. From 1674 to 1676, colonials fought with Indians of the Wampanoag and other cultures in northern Rhode Island, southeastern and central Massachusetts, and in some scattered settlements in northern Connecticut. Among dozens of points of engagement, conflict took place in Bridgewater, Middleborough, the Pocasset Swamp near Fall River, and in Medfield. The war resulted in the decimation and uprooting of tribal groups throughout the three states and in the confiscation of their lands.

Leave MA 105 here, *bearing right and southeast* on MA 28 at 19.8 miles. MA 28 rolls past playing fields, open marsh, and woodlands as it drops southeast, becoming gradually more rural. You pass the Old Colony YMCA at 20.5 miles and then cross Fall Brook. Go by hidden Tispaquin Pond on the left shortly, and *watch for Rocky Gutter Street*, also on the left, onto which you will turn at 23.8 miles.

This leg of the trip runs through Rocky Gutter Wildlife Management Area on the street of the same name, a real woods experience where you will need to slow down on an occasionally rough right-of-way. The woods here, thick with white pines, beech, spotted alder, and greenbriar, are a nice contrast to the open country driven through earlier. The road wends its way through two great, swampy lowlands, the larger, to the right, known as South Purchase Swamp. Emerging on the other side of the marsh you *go left* on France Street at a T.

At 28.1 miles, rolling northeast, you round an enormous cranberry bog and cross into Carver. Pass a serene little pond on the left that feeds the Weweantic River and come to Popes Point Road, where you *go right and southeast* through marsh and cultivated cranberry bogs, crossing South Meadow Brook. The route intersects Meadow Street shortly, where you *keep left* for Carver center. You emerge at a T intersection with MA 58 in Carver soon, and then *go right* toward South Carver. Here you're in the heart of what have been traditionally the largest cranberry-producing grounds in eastern America.

Coming into South Carver, you take the curves between two attractive large ponds and then leave MA 58, *going left and northeast* onto Tremont Street. On Tremont, opposite Sampson Pond, watch for Cranberry Road on the right, where you *turn eastward.* Cross West Line Road while skirting another open bog and, continuing east, come to Myles Standish State Forest Headquarters in groves of tall white pines at roughly 37 miles.[*] Go left and northeast here, going around lovely Head Pond, where there are beautiful views over the water to your right at 37.8 miles. At 38 miles *keep left* at a junction marked Curlew Pond and then *left and north* at another junction. The road next climbs steadily left and right over a series of ribs toward the north-northeast as it narrows in groves of densely grown jack pine on ground elevated well above the boglands traveled earlier.

Skirt Rocky Pond to the left and join Rocky Pond Road at 41.2 miles,

---

[*] Within Myles Standish State Forest, it's easy to lose the thread of travel in the tangle of wandering roads, many of which are not well marked. There are also many park roads not noted on typical maps of the region. If you get off the route described here, you cannot go wrong if you simply continue northward once in the park. You will eventually emerge on the park's north side on the outskirts of Plymouth. If you get lost, ask for directions at park headquarters (open seasonally).

continuing generally northward. Pass Widgeon Pond Road at 41.4 miles and enjoy fine views rightward over the pond. You go past South Curlew Pond Road, just beyond, and the return loop of Widgeon Pond Road again at roughly 42 miles. These small, pretty bodies of water are pleasant interruptions in the continuous thick, low jack-pine forest, offering refreshment to the jaded eye. You crest Pinnacle Hill and come to several houses at 43 miles, passing another cranberry bog to the left, then descending in hardwood groves on a street called, simply, Watercourse. Here there are more extensive water views to the right and through the trees, just before you pass Drew Road.

Watercourse becomes Billington Street as you continue traveling north-northeast through more low ground approaching Plymouth, then reaching a more settled area punctuated by wooded bogs. There are further pond views at 45 miles as you go by the interestingly named Billington Sea, and the route dips narrowly between two hillsides beyond which you drive under MA 3 and along a pretty, flooded marsh. You enter another residential neighborhood now, following a little brook where you pass a picnic area. Billington joins Summer Street in moments at 46.5 miles, and you follow Summer Street eastward into town. Passing the old Grist Mill on the right, Summer Street will deposit you right in Plymouth center where this drive ends at a T with Main Street (MA 3A). 🏃

19

Route
Sagamore to Orleans

Highway
MA 6A

Distance
36 miles plus local excursions

Here is the first of two easterly drives that take in the best of Cape Cod terrain. The north shore of the Cape, as we will travel it, is a place of attractive small communities that still display some of the unique natural hallmarks that have made this a fabled place much written about and assiduously visited for more than one hundred fifty years. Modern Cape Cod's south shore, on the other hand, has become a less appealing clutter of trinket shops, motels, and other visual offenses, and should be avoided. Though the south shore is ostensibly a place to go to enjoy the Atlantic coast, there are few places along the Cape's main southern highway where one can even *see* the ocean, given the wall-to-wall motels, eateries, and stores. Also, MA 28 between Hyannis and Chatham in high summer is home to more or less continuous traffic congestion. As we'll see, however, there *are* still inviting places to drive in the Cape's northern and western precincts, and they are described in this chapter and the following one.

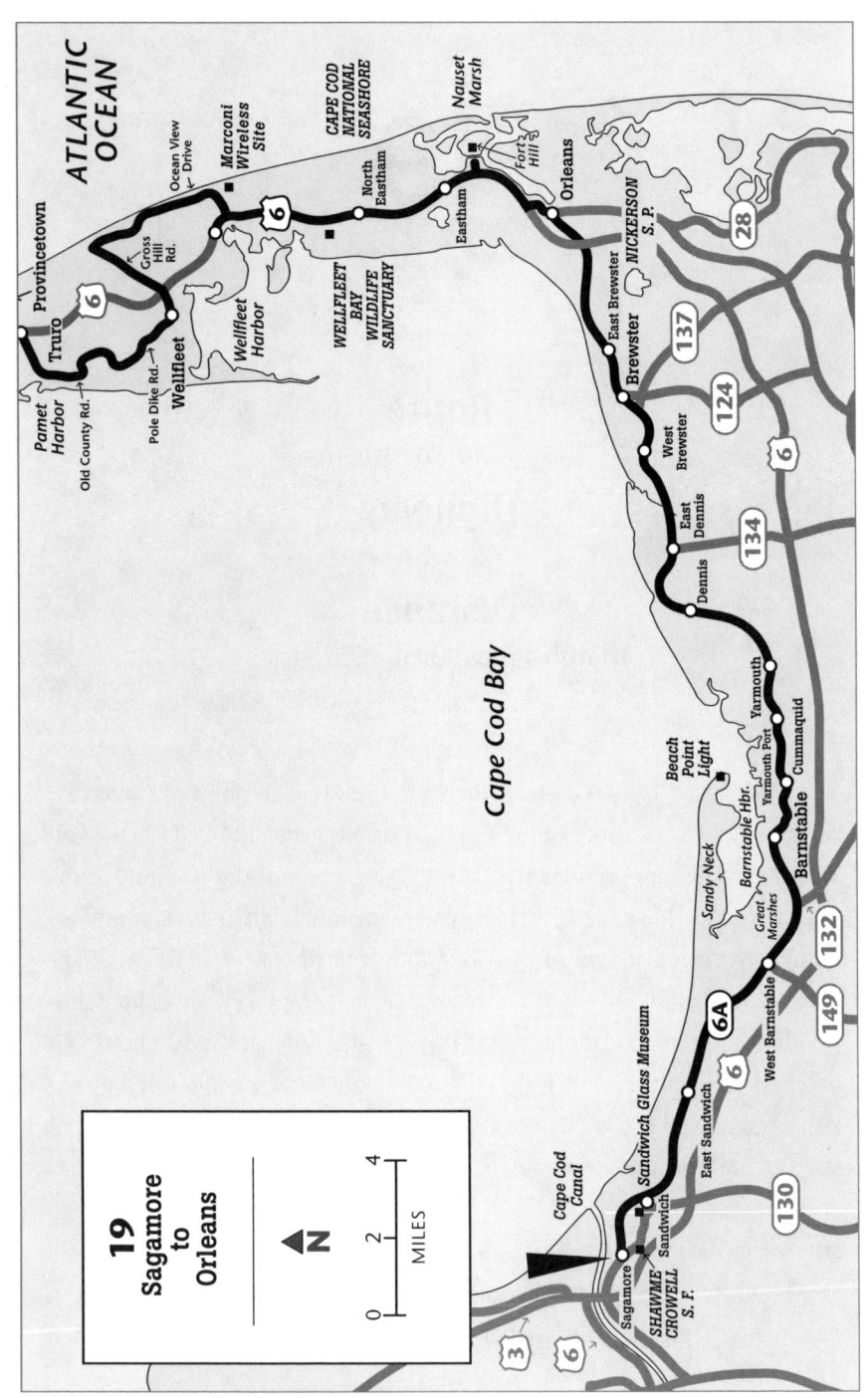

**19
Sagamore
to
Orleans**

N

MILES

0   2   4

ATLANTIC
OCEAN

Provincetown

Truro

Pamet Harbor

Old County Rd.

Pole Dike Rd.

Wellfleet

Wellfleet Harbor

Gross Hill Rd.

Ocean View Drive

Marconi Wireless Site

CAPE COD NATIONAL SEASHORE

North Eastham

WELLFLEET BAY WILDLIFE SANCTUARY

Eastham

Nauset Marsh

Fort Hill

Orleans

6

6

6

Cape Cod Bay

NICKERSON S. P.

East Brewster

Brewster

137

124

West Brewster

6

134

East Dennis

Dennis

28

Yarmouth

Yarmouth Port

Cummaquid

Beach Point Light

Barnstable Hbr.

Barnstable

Sandy Neck

Great Marshes

132

149

West Barnstable

6A

6

Sandwich Glass Museum

East Sandwich

130

Cape Cod Canal

Sandwich

Sagamore

SHAWME CROWELL S. F.

3

6

Sagamore to Orleans

An interesting drive along the Cape's north shore begins in Sagamore at the Bourne Bridge by the Cape Cod Canal. Pick up MA 6A *east* under the bridge (Exit 1 from MA 3) and head toward Sandwich on the route of what was once the King's Highway. The road swings through a residential area north of Shawme Crowell State Forest, goes through a junction with MA 130 at 1.9 miles, and then follows the marshes that back Sandwich Harbor to the north. Church steeples rise above the trees and marsh ahead, and a side road leads right to the interesting Sandwich Glass Museum, which is worth a visit.

In his *Cape Cod Yesterdays*, Joseph Lincoln argued that there was at least one prominent Cape industry that hadn't much to do with the sea, namely glass making, and that lay right here in Sandwich. The sea did furnish the raw material even in this instance, Lincoln allowed, for "away back in the beginning of things, [the sea] pushed and washed up from its bed the clean, flinty sand, the abundance of which was the primary cause of the factory's locating on that site, and, in the days before the railway, the product was, much of it, sent away in sailing craft . . . glassware of all kinds and descriptions."

You pass the connector to the Massachusetts Fish Hatchery at 4.1 miles, going eastward through Sandwich center. The road gets out into more open country soon, bordered by clumps of locust and hobblebush viburnum, with more bogland, busy with shorebirds, to the right at 5.6 miles. The route next goes through a neighborhood known as the Springs, passes a conservation area on the left at 7.4 miles, and continues along the edge of a broad salt marsh to the left and north as it goes by Plowed Neck and comes to East Sandwich. Here the road follows Scorton Creek on the right and passes several streets to the left that connect with Sandy Neck and Scorton Neck. Sandy Neck—a great, narrow barrier beach capped by Beach Point Light—forms the north wall of Barnstable Harbor. Passing a marsh to the south, you cross Scorton Brook, which feeds the Great Marshes on this end of Barnstable Harbor. Head

The Marconi Wireless Site, outer Cape Cod

over the Barnstable line at 9.5 miles and drive past Scorton Hill, with the marshes to the north now, screened by spotted alder, dense-grown greenbriar, and viburnum.

You pass through West Barnstable village and a junction with MA 149 next. Cross the rail line and then Bridge Creek. Splendid views of the seemingly endless Great Marshes appear on the left at 12.3 miles. Here you jump over another creek that connects the marshes and harbor with Garretts Pond, lying inland and to the right. Pass the Cottage-style First Lutheran Church and come to a junction with MA 132 at 13.3 miles, where you *stay left* on 6A, next running northeast.

As it winds and bends now, 6A makes its way parallel to the Cape's northern perimeter, passing some pleasant old Federal and Greek Revival houses as it rolls through Pond Village. The route then pulls more eastward and arrives at the county courthouse in Barnstable proper at 15.7

miles, with the Town of Barnstable Museum just beyond. Barnstable proves an inviting town in the old Cape tradition, with attractive older homes, varied shops, eating places, and inns.

Continuing eastward, you drive next through Cummaquid, where side streets on the left offer cross-harbor views of Beach Point Light. Enter Yarmouth at 18.4 miles and go through the little neighborhood known as Yarmouth Port, a place of inns and galleries, where the Captain Bangs-Hallett House and Winslow-Crocker House (1780) are two of several historic sites of interest. Off to the north are the Bass Hole Marshes, while patchy, thick hardwood groves lie to the south.

As you approach Dennis, 6A then pulls more to the northeast and then north, drifting inland a little to skirt the boggy Black Flats and Chase Garden Creek. Galleries and antiques shops signal cozy Dennis village, where you ride by a bandstand and the Union Church at just over 23 miles. The Cape Playhouse Center for the Arts is here also.

Now you pass Seaside Avenue, where you'll graze the Atlantic shore near Nobscusset Point, then drift southeasterly around pretty Sargo Pond to your right, pulling inland again, to go through East Dennis. Signs indicate Indian burial grounds in this area, testament to its earliest residents, here long before European arrivals. High grasses screen the marsh leftward and woodlands dominated by jack pines lie rightward at 25.4 miles as you go farther east, passing a junction with MA 134.

You'll cross into West Brewster next, following Quivett Creek as it descends northward to the marshes of the same name at Quivett Point. The road dips inland and then climbs northeastward again to West Brewster center, at 28 miles. The coastal Museum of Natural History is found here, surrounded by beautiful marsh views. Going through a junction with MA 137, come into Brewster village by the Trinity Lutheran Church and the town's attractive, old-style, clapboarded library.

A century ago, the distance between Brewster and Boston was formidable, the problematic cart track known as the King's Highway being an inefficient way to carry produce to market and to bring essentials back to the outer Cape. The solution was an estimable schooner known as the *Brewster Packet*. It became one of several packet boats that ran between Barnstable, Dennis, Yarmouth, and Boston, saving a lot of rough overland travel. A pole erected on nearby Canon Hill sported a hoist beacon that indicated when the packet was ashore.

In a section dotted with shops and galleries, you pass MA 124 on the right at 30.3 miles and then drive through East Brewster, north of hidden Blueberry Pond. Broad Cape Cod Bay lies just a block away down several side streets to the left, while patches of woodland dominate the view to the south. Passing the Brewster Historical Society Museum at 32.8 miles and the Cape Cod Rail Trail Scenic Area just beyond, you shortly reach superb Nickerson State Park, with its lovely kettle hole pond, at 33.3 miles. There are pleasant facilities here for camping and swimming, plus trails for walking. Nickerson is a perennially popular destination for outdoor types, and campers should make reservations early for July and August.

Marsh views to the left yield to a built-up area of antiques shops and galleries as you cross into Orleans at 34.7 miles. Rock Harbor Road, to the left, leads to fine views of the working waterfront and the bay. Go under MA 6 and follow 6A to its junction with MA 28 in Orleans at 36.1 miles, where this drive ends.

Want more? There are some further driving possibilities for those who wish to explore the "hook" of Cape Cod beyond Orleans. One obvious choice is to drive all the way to Provincetown at the tip of the Cape. The famous little community—proud home to fishermen, but now also to many artists, writers, sometime dramatists, and other creative types—is eminently worth a visit, especially in late spring and early summer and also when the season winds down after Labor Day. In high summer, the tangled little streets of P-town are crowded, congested, and not much fun

 Nauset Marsh

to drive. Plan accordingly. If you visit Provincetown, take time to first turn right as you approach town and look in on the Provincelands Trails network and the Old Harbor Lifesaving Museum, both on Race Point Road. (See the author's *Weekend Walks on the New England Coast* for information.)

If you don't wish to brave MA 6 all the way to Provincetown on a hot summer day, a more interesting drive wends north on alternating west and east fringes of the Cape through Eastham and Wellfleet to Truro. From Orleans, *drive north on MA 6* to Eastham and visit the Cape Cod National Seashore's historic Nauset Marsh area before proceeding to the Wellfleet Bay Wildlife Sanctuary in North Eastham. Continuing on to South Wellfleet, *bear right* on Oceanview Drive for a cruise along the Cape Cod National Seashore, passing the Marconi Wireless Site, from which President Theodore Roosevelt's pioneering telegraph message was sent across the Atlantic to England's Edward VII in 1903. Follow Ocean-view Drive, going through Wellfleet-by-the-Sea, and *return west toward MA 6* via Gross Hill Road.

Crossing MA 6 to Wellfleet center, *go west* on Pole Dike Road, taking in the Wellfleet Historical Society Museum and the National Seashore's Great Island nature area. An outstanding network of walking trails traverses Great Island and Great Beach Hill, leading to spectacular views of Cape Cod Bay and Jeremy Point. Pole Dike Road winds north through the marshes, crossing the Herring River and Bound Brook, and becomes Old County Road as it passes Pamet Harbor and then arches northeast into Truro.

20

Route
Sagamore to South Cape Beach

Highway
MA 6A, 130, Great Neck Road

Distance
23.5 miles

This shorter drive makes its way across the west-central region of Cape Cod, linking the north shore with the south, traversing the jack-pine scrub woods of the Cape's center and reaching its end by the beautiful Waquoit Bay National Estuarine Reserve in the Cape's southwest corner. The route offers a means to visit the interior community of Mashpee, a state forest, a state park, and a superb sand beach.

Begin at the Sagamore Bridge over the Cape Cod Canal, where MA 6 and 6A intersect. Go under the bridge and *pick up MA 6A*, which you follow *east* for less than two miles. Cross the Sandwich line and *bear right* on MA 130 shortly (set your odometer to zero here), and head southeast, where you come almost immediately to Shawme Crowell State Forest. There are excellent picnicking and camping facilities here—with 89 individual sites, showers, hiking trails, and a nature study area—in a park that remains open year-round for hardy types. One of the great virtues of the Cape, after all, is its moderate winter climate.

Sunset at South Cape Beach State Park

Pass the colonnaded Sandwich Town Hall at 2.2 miles by a mill dam, and just beyond it the Thornton W. Burgess Museum, commemorating the prolific writer of nature books for children. Watch for signs here, too, for the Sandwich Glass Museum, an interesting look at American glass-making artifacts from the 1800s onward, with emphasis on glass forms produced locally. The Boston and Sandwich Glassworks had its start in 1825, founded by Deming Jarves, who bought up two thousand acres of local pine woodland to feed the new kiln. The works turned out both articles for the masses and pieces by individual "gaffers," the relics of which are much treasured today. Reaching its heyday in the mid-1850s, the works closed in 1888.

MA 130 next pulls southward where you pass a side road to the right. This road leads to the Heritage Plantation, a living history display featuring things well preserved, old, and older. The route skirts a lake to the

Sagamore to South Cape Beach

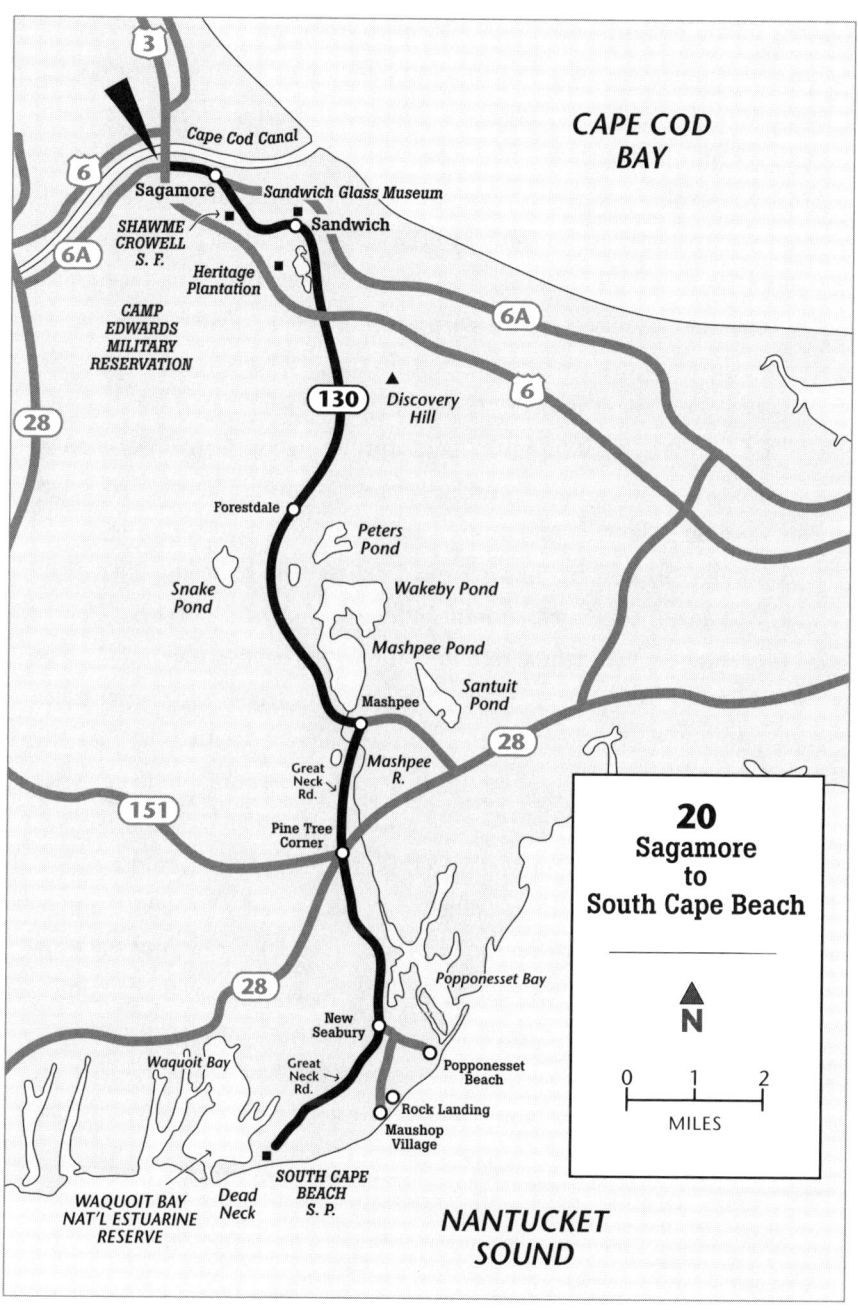

CAPE COD BAY

③

Cape Cod Canal

⑥

Sagamore   Sandwich Glass Museum

SHAWME
CROWELL
S. F.   Sandwich

⑥A

Heritage
Plantation

CAMP
EDWARDS
MILITARY
RESERVATION

⑥A

②⑧

▲
130   Discovery
Hill

⑥

Forestdale

Peters
Pond

Snake
Pond   Wakeby Pond

Mashpee Pond

Santuit
Pond

Mashpee

②⑧

Great
Neck
Rd.   Mashpee
R.

①⑤①

Pine Tree
Corner

②⑧

Popponesset Bay

New
Seabury

Great
Neck
Rd.   Popponesset
Beach

Waquoit Bay

Rock Landing
Maushop
Village

SOUTH CAPE
BEACH
S. P.

WAQUOIT BAY
NAT'L ESTUARINE
RESERVE   Dead
Neck

NANTUCKET
SOUND

20
Sagamore
to
South Cape Beach

▲
N

0   1   2

MILES

right and rolls farther southward through a second section of Shawme
Crowell State Forest. In a moment you pass under MA 6 and rise southeast toward Forestdale in dense jack-pine scrub as you follow the edge of
the old Camp Edwards Military Reservation, now the home of the Otis
Army National Guard Center. The route drops south some more in continuous woodlands broken only by occasional development as it runs opposite Discovery Hill off to the east. The hill is one of several promonto-
ries that mark a raised rib down the center of the Cape's sandy arch,
though elevation here is more perception than reality. One of the highest
points on the Cape, Discovery Hill soars a mere 260 feet upward.

Pass Cotuit Road at 5.4 miles, and roll through attractive woodlands.
The drive now pulls more southwest through Forestdale between Peters
Pond and Snake Pond. An entrance to the military reservation is passed
at 8.1 miles. You go by Snake Pond Road on the right and then head
southeast again, going next around hidden Wakeby and Mashpee Ponds.

One might argue that the terrain of the Cape resembles a kind of Swiss
cheese, its surface pocked with dozens of small lakes and ponds like
these, the result of glacial scouring and subsequent weathering. Actually,
there are more than twenty ponds of varying size within a mile or two of
this route as it progresses. (See the author's *Weekend Walks on the New
England Coast* for pondside walks in this area.) Cape Codder Joseph Lincoln reminisced about these waters in his *Cape Cod Yesterdays*: "A good
many of the larger ponds on the Cape are called lakes now, but the Cape
Cod of earlier generations had not a lake on it. They were all ponds."
Many of the ponds fed streams that, in season, became flush with herring, and locals came to capture the teeming fish when the runs were on.
Lincoln reported that a typical herring stream was, at such moments,
"filled for two-thirds of its depth with silver—silver that is alive, that
leaps and flaps and is never still. And in the midst of this—buried almost
to the knees in glistening fish—is a rubber-booted man with a dip-net,
who bends to scoop netful after netful of herring. . . ."

**Nauset Beach Light,
outer Cape Cod**

You cross the Mashpee town line at 8.5 miles in acres of scrub oak and then pass the 4-H Outdoor Education Center on the left at 9.8 miles. There are several signs in this zone indicating ancient tribal lands of the Wampanoag tribe. Mashpee formally came to be in a series of land trades with the original Indian settlers, when Miles Standish purchased an enormous tract of Cape land in 1648 in exchange for two brass kettles and a bushel of Indian corn. Uncomfortable with this legalized swindle, preacher Richard Bourne later split off a part of his lands here to accommodate the Mashpee tribe, thus averting a conflict. The Indians would have to send a representative to London to beg for and attain eventual self-government. Mashpee Indians also fought and died on the side of the Americans in the Revolution and were then promptly repaid by having their self-governing status revoked by the patriots. Freedom, the erstwhile colonials had decided, was not suitable for just anyone.

Go by Ashumet Road on the right at 10.3 miles and then cross the Mashpee River, where you'll have limited views left to attractive Mashpee Pond. Here you reach the center of Mashpee, where you leave MA 130 at 11 miles. *Bear right* by the Mashpee Town Hall onto Great Neck Road and go south again, crossing the Mashpee River a second time in a marshy area, then following it south in sandy Cape ground thick with jack pines.

You soon cross old Barnstable Road and move next through a more developed neighborhood to Pine Tree Corner. The "corner," really a five-way rotary, is reached at 13.5 miles. Watch carefully here for Great Neck Road on the far side, where you depart *south* again toward South Cape Beach State Park.

The next leg of this western Cape trip runs down the map to the southeast, where the Mashpee River widens as it enters Popponesset Bay and Ockway Bay. There are intriguing bay views to the left as you descend onto what is known as Great Neck. From a crossroads called New Seabury, a connector road departs left for Popponesset Beach, Rock Landing, and Maushop Village. As you continue straight ahead, heading southwest now, the Great Neck Road soon follows the eastern fringe of the National Estuarine Research Reserve, a series of protected lands in two counties surrounding Waquoit Bay.

Watch now for signs indicating the entrance to South Cape Beach State Park and follow the narrow road to a parking area near the water's edge at roughly 23.5 miles. Here is the Cape as much of it once was—a striking, unspoiled border of sand and rolling surf, with the broad expanse of Nantucket Sound stretched out in front of you as far as the eye can see. Dead Neck lies to the right, and an invigorating stroll, summer or winter, is possible all the way west to the point where the Atlantic enters Waquoit Bay. A walk of some length can be done in the opposite direction toward Maushop Village, too. And, if you've timed your drive just so, the sunsets here can be spectacular.

Appendix A
An Author's Favorites

One of the great pleasures of back roads travel throughout the Bay State is the almost unending selection of good places to rest one's head. The tradition of hostelry here dates back to the nation's founding, and you will find comfortable places to pause in every region. Variety is the key word. Whether you prefer larger, modern hotel facilities with all the amenities or smaller, traditional guests houses and inns, Massachusetts offers much to satisfy back-roads travelers. While on the more than 3,500-mile driving odyssey that led to this book, I enjoyed a rest in the hotels, inns, and guesthouses noted below. I think you will too.

In southeastern Massachusetts it was a pleasure to find Kathy Reed's **Edgewater Bed and Breakfast** establishment on the banks of the broad Achushnet River in Fairhaven. Originally built as a store by Elnathan Eldridge in 1760 and expanded by Bostonian Clara Anthony in the 1880s, Edge-

Edgewater Bed and Breakfast

water is now a modern, comfortable guesthouse with the well-preserved flavor of an old New England merchant's home. Fireplaces, water views, and period furnishings make this a delightful haven. Edgewater, on what has been called Poverty Point, looks across the Acushnet to one-time whaling capital New Bedford, with its museums and other attractions. For those who prefer quiet, traditional surroundings with thoughtful attention to details, Edgewater is a natural choice.

Edgewater Bed and Breakfast

2 Oxford Street

Fairhaven, MA 02179

Tel. (508) 997-5512

www.rixsan.com/edgewater/

In historic Concord, not far from the Revolution's famous Battle Green and Thoreau's Walden Pond, those fond of accommodation in historic surroundings will favor a stay in Concord's **Colonial Inn,** situated at the north end of Monument Square. The inn has kept its original flavor, occupying three old buildings dating from 1716. This structure was early home to Revolutionary War physician Dr. Timothy Minot. Henry David Thoreau's grandfather, John Thoreau, acquired the house in 1799. Henry himself lived in this place from 1835 to 1837 while attending Harvard College. A store was operated here, too, before 1850, and one can still imagine the street out front busy with the horse carts of customers and loiterers. The structure has been formally an inn since the late 1800s, and today it provides comfortable modern amenities within an historic setting.

The Colonial Inn

48 Monument Square

Concord, MA 01742

Tel. (978) 369-9200

www.concordscolonialinn.com

Appendix A: An Author's Favorites

The Brandt House

In north-central Massachusetts, a special discovery is the Phoebe Compton's **Brandt House**. This elegant sixteen-room estate situated on Greenfield's wooded east side provides quiet, welcoming accommodation in period surroundings reminiscent of the days when this fine colonial-revival structure was home to a leading area physician and his family. The Brandt House's extensive grounds include sloping lawns and tennis courts overlooked by a shaded breakfast court. Inside, the marvelous original features of the structure have been preserved in beautiful native woods. Several rooms have fireplaces, and breakfast is always pleasant in the sunny dining room. Walks to Greenfield's famous Poet's Seat are found nearby.

The Brandt House
29 Highland Avenue
Greenfield, MA 01301
Tel. (800) 235-3329 or (413) 774-3329

Salem, founded in 1626 and originally named Naumkeag, is a marvelous stopping-off place for North Shore travelers. Here the attractive **Salem Inn**, in the heart of Old Salem, invites you to sample fine accommodations associated with an earlier time. It consists of the bold, brick-fronted Captain West House, the colonnaded, Federal-style Curwen House, and the 1874 Peabody House. At rates lower than most found in nearby Boston, the Salem Inn offers 42 rooms decorated in eighteenth- and nineteenth-century fashion, grand breakfasts, and a window on how people lived in this famous seaport centuries ago. Many of the rooms have fireplaces.

Close by are the interesting Salem Maritime National Historic Site, the fascinating and indispensable Peabody Essex Museum, the Witch House, the Salem 1620 Pioneer Village, and the Salem Witch Museum. Nathaniel Hawthorne lived here, working as local Collector of Customs and gaining inspiration to write *The House of the Seven Gables*.

The Salem Inn

7 Summer Street, Salem, MA 01970.

Tel. (978) 741-0680

On-line at www.SalemInnMa.com

e-mail, salem.inn@verizon.net

All the latest contemporary decor and services await guests at the **Royal Plaza Hotel** in Fitchburg. A member of the Best Western system, the Royal Plaza offers 245 rooms of varying size and is situated immediately ad-jacent to the Royal Plaza Trade Center, a forum for trade shows, conferences, and regional meetings. Built around an attractive open atrium, the hotel boasts its own restaurant and lounge, pool, fitness room, jacuzzi, and sauna. Manager Francis Tuscano welcomes guests to this spotless full-service hostelry just off Route 2, Massachusetts's major east-west artery for the Berkshires and hill country.

The Royal Plaza Hotel

150 Royal Plaza Drive

Fitchburg, MA 01420-6024

Tel. (978) 343-7376 or (888) 976-9254

Appendix A: An Author's Favorites

✦ The **Clarion Inn at Northampton** delivers all the modern comforts in the heart of the interesting and inviting five-college area. The inn lies unobtrusively back from MA 5 about 2.5 miles south of Northampton's center. A breakfast service greets guests in the morning, and the indoor pool provides a refreshing way to relax after a day on the road. The inn is a good base for exploration of the campuses of the five colleges and the pretty west-central Massachusetts countryside.

> The Clarion Inn at Northampton
> 1 Atwood Drive (off MA Route 5)
> Northampton, MA 01060
> Tel. (413) 586-1211

✦ **Old Sturbridge Village Lodges** and the **Oliver Wright House**, in the heart of colonial Sturbridge, welcome guests who are just passing through or stopping a while when visiting the area's numerous attractions. The Oliver Wright House was constructed in 1789 and became a landmark local tavern and hostelry. It offers ten beautiful rooms in welcoming Federal style. Old Sturbridge Village Lodges make a good jumping-off place for local pastimes.

Sturbridge and surrounds offer lots to do whatever the season: summer concerts on numerous village greens, the Brimfield Antiques Show, a fall Harvest Festival, flea markets, apple picking at local orchards, and, of course, a whole range of events at Old Sturbridge Village itself. The Village Lodges provide all the comforts expected by the weary traveler, and more, and families touring the magnificent Sturbridge restoration will find this a natural place to stay.

> Old Sturbridge Village Lodges
> One Old Sturbridge Village Road
> Sturbridge, MA 01566
> Tel. (508) 347-3327

🏃The **Belfry Inne and Bistro** in Sandwich, Massachusetts, just off MA 6A, is a true find and, hands-down, one of the most inviting places to stay or dine on the Cape. Owner Christopher Wilson has converted an old church rectory and adjacent Victorian home into a premier-class bed-and-breakfast and restaurant. Both structures offer elegant, exceptionally well decorated rooms. In the Abbey, the dining room, with its soaring, buttressed ceilings and colorful interior,

The Belfry Inne

is home to the imaginative cuisine of Brazilian-born Chef Argos Pilo. Across the courtyard, Drew House with its own lofty tower, has been restored to a certain high-gingerbread Victorian glory. These two buildings, together, are the Belfry Inne and Bistro, and no better example exists of intelligent preservation of existing structures, giving them new life as a grand stopping place for discerning Cape Cod visitors. Plan your Cape journey around a stay here and book ahead.

The Belfry Inne and Bistro
6–8 Jarves Street, PO Box 2211
Sandwich, MA 02563
Tel. (508) 888-8550 or (800) 844-4542
On line: www.belfryinn.com
e-mail: info@belfryinn.com

➤On the waterfront in Gloucester, right in the midst of things aquatic, is the **Cape Ann Marina Resort**, a great informal stopover, especially if you are traveling with a family or are warm to boating. Located about as close to seaward as you can get and still be on land, the Marina Resort rises in the midst of wharfs and docks busy with charters, mooring traffic, and private dockage. The Resort's 52 rooms look out over the channel that connects Ipswich Bay to the north with Gloucester Harbor, giving this destination a decidedly salty flavor. A swimming pool, hot tubs, dining room, and other amenities make this a place where you might want to remain for days without wandering. Charter fishing, diving, and whale-watching cruises depart from here, too. Famous Cape Ann beaches are nearby.

The Cape Ann Marina Resort

75 Essex Avenue (MA Rte. 133)

Gloucester, MA 01930

Tel. (978) 283-2116 or nationally (800) 626-7660

Appendix B
Sources of
Useful Information

To obtain a copy of the *Massachusetts Getaway Guide*, contact:

> The Massachusetts Office of Travel and Tourism
> 10 Park Plaza, Suite 4510
> Boston, MA 02116
> Tel. (800) 227-MASS
> www.massvacation.com

Regional Travel Information Centers

Greater Boston Convention and Visitors Bureau
(617) 536-4100 or (888) SEE BOSTON

North of Boston Convention and Visitors Bureau
(Peabody)
(978) 977-7760 or (800) 742-5306

Greater Merrimack Valley Convention and
Visitors Bureau (Lowell)
(978) 459-6150 or (800) 443-3332

Appendix B: Sources of Useful Information

Bristol County Convention and Visitors Bureau
(Southeastern Massachusetts)
(508) 997-1250 or (800) 288-6263

Plymouth County Convention and Visitors Bureau
(South Shore)
(508) 747-0100 or (800) 231-1620

Cape Cod Chamber of Commerce
(508) 862-0700 or (800) 33CapeCod

Central Massachusetts Tourist Council
(508) 755-7400

Greater Springfield Convention and Visitors Bureau
(413) 787-1548 or (800) 723-1548

Franklin County Chamber of Commerce
(Northwestern Massachusetts)
(413) 773-5463

Berkshire Visitors Bureau
(413) 443-9186 or (800) 237-5747

Trails and Wildlife Sanctuaries

For information on managed trail sites and wildlife sanctuaries
in Massachusetts, contact:

The Massachusetts Department of
Environmental Management
(617) 626-1250

The Trustees of Reservations
(978) 921-1944

The Massachusetts Audubon Society
(781) 259-9500

The Appalachian Mountain Club
(413) 443-0011

National Historic Parks and Natural Areas in Massachusetts

For information on national historic parks, the Cape Cod National Seashore, and national recreation areas in Massachusetts, contact:

The National Park Service
(888) GOPARKS

Massachusetts State Parks

For information on Massachusetts State Parks, individual park facilities, and information on park reservations, contact:

The Massachusetts Department of Environmental Management
(617) 626-1250.
Request the publication, *Massachusetts Forests and Recreational Activities.*
Call (877) 422-6762 to place campsite reservations.

Private Campgrounds

For information on private campgrounds in Massachusetts and their facilities, contact:

The Massachusetts Association of Campground Owners
(781) 544-3475